The Way Things Aren't

RUSH LIMBAUGH'S REIGN OF ERROR

Over 100 outrageously false and foolish statements
from America's most powerful radio and TV commentator

Written for FAIR by
Steven Rendall, Jim Naureckas, and Jeff Cohen

THE NEW PRESS
NEW YORK

YOUR MIND IS ON VACATION

You know if talk was criminal,
You'd lead a life of crime.
Because your mind is on vacation,
And your mouth is workin' overtime.

You're quotin' figures and droppin' names,
You're tellin' stories about the dames,
You're always laughin' when things ain't funny,
You're tryin' to sound like big money.
You know if silence was golden,
You couldn't raise a dime.
—Mose Allison (© 1961, Audre Mae Music)

© 1995 by FAIR

LIBRARY OF CONGRESS CATALOGING-IN-PUBLICATION DATA

Rendall, Steven.
     The way things aren't: Rush Limbaugh's reign of error: over 100 outrageously false and foolish
statements from America's most powerful radio and TV commentator / written for FAIR by Steven
Rendall, Jim Naureckas, and Jeff Cohen.
     p.   cm.
     ISBN 1-56584-260-X
     1. Limbaugh, Rush H.—Quotations. I. Limbaugh, Rush H. II. Naureckas, Jim. III. Cohen, Jeff.
IV. Fairness & Accuracy In Reporting (Organization). V. Title.
PN1991.4.L48R47   1995
791.44'028'092—dc20   94-46494

Published in the United States by The New Press, New York
Distributed by W. W. Norton & Company, Inc., New York, NY 10110

Established in 1990 as a major alternative to the large, commercial publishing houses, The New Press is the first full-scale nonprofit American
book publisher outside of the university presses. The Press is operated editorially in the public interest, rather than for private gain; it is
committed to publishing in innovative ways works of educational, cultural, and community value that, despite their intellectual merits, might
not normally be commercially viable. The New Press's editorial offices are located at the City University of New York.

Book design by Laura Lindgren
Production management by Kim Waymer
Printed in the United States of America

95 96 97 98   9 8 7 6 5 4 3 2 1

CONTENTS

FOREWORD

by Molly Ivins

Austin, Texas

One of the things that has concerned me lately is an increase in plain old nastiness in political discussion. It comes from many sources, but Rush Limbaugh is a prime example.

I should explain that I am not without bias in this matter. I have been attacked on the air by Rush Limbaugh. It's an experience somewhat akin to being gummed by a newt. It does not actually hurt, but it leaves you with slimy stuff on your ankle.

I have a correspondent named Irwin Wingo in Weatherford, Texas. Irwin and some of the leading men in the town are in the habit, about ten o'clock in the morning, of meeting down at the cafe to drink coffee and talk about the state of the world. One of the members of their group is a dittohead, a great Limbaugh listener. He came in one day, plopped himself down, and said, "You know, Rush is right: Racism is dead in this country. I don't know what the niggers have to gripe about now."

I wouldn't say that dittoheads as a group lack the ability to reason. It's just that when I run across them, they seem to be at a low ebb in reasoning skills.

In my state, not since the heyday of the John Birch Society in the early 1960s have I seen so much hatred in politics. Used to be you couldn't talk about politics with a conservative without their getting all red in the face, veins standing out in their necks. They'd look like angry turkey gobblers. Now I've found that anger again.

The kind of humor Limbaugh uses is something that I have been much troubled about, because I've spent my professional life making fun of politicians. It's a great American tradition and should be encouraged. We should all laugh at these guys. So what right do I have to object, just because Limbaugh laughs at them and not the ones I do?

Because satire can be quite a cruel weapon. It has historically been the weapon of powerless people aimed at the powerful. When you use satire as a weapon against powerless people, it is not only cruel, it is profoundly vulgar. It is very much like kicking a cripple.

When I listen to Limbaugh, as I often do, I find he consistently targets dead people, little girls, the homeless, and animals—none of whom are in a particularly good position to respond. It is the consistency of his selection of helpless targets that I find so appalling.

On his TV show in 1993, he put up a picture of Socks, the White House cat, and said: "Did you know there's a White House dog?" And then he put up a picture of Chelsea Clinton, who was 13 years old and as far as I know had never done any harm to anyone.

Then of course, in Limbaugh-like fashion, he claims that it had been an accident and that without his permission some technician on his show did that. Which I found almost as disgusting as the original attempt at humor.

I also think that he has a somewhat cultlike effect on his followers. They listen to him for three and a half hours a day on radio and television. I am in a position to assure you that David Koresh did not talk to the Branch Davidians that much. But that is precisely what cult leaders do: They talk to their followers hour after hour after hour.

The reason I take Limbaugh seriously is not because he's offensive or right wing. It's because I think he speaks to a large group of disaffected people in this country. A big part of Limbaugh's audience are white males 18 to 34 years old, many without a college education. Basically that's a guy I knew and grew up with named Bubba.

The reason Bubba listens to Limbaugh is because Limbaugh gives Bubba somebody to blame for the fact that he, Bubba, is getting screwed. And he is. Bubba's working hard and not only is he not getting ahead, he's falling further and further behind. He can barely afford the payments on the pickup.

It is because Bubba has a very real sense of being shafted that I think Limbaugh is worth listening to. What he's doing is giving Bubba somebody to blame. It's feminazis. It's the minorities. It's the limousine liberals. It's all these people with all these wacky social programs to help some kind of silly self-proclaimed wounded bunch.

Psychologists say there's a great deal of displaced anger in our emotional lives. It's also very common in our political life. We see it in a generation of fairly young white men with no future at all. This economy no longer has a place for them. Unfortunately, it is Limbaugh and his people who are talking to those folks and aiming their anger in the wrong direction.

MY FRIENDS, RECENTLY THE FEMINAZIS AND WACKOS AT "FAIR" ISSUED A REPORT QUESTIONING THE ACCURACY OF SOME OF MY STATEMENTS. WHY? BECAUSE THEY **RESENT** THE STRAIGHT TALK ON MY SHOWS!

WHO ELSE HAS HAD THE GUTS TO TALK ABOUT VINT FOSTER'S 1992 MURDER IN ROOSEVELT PARK ONLY **DAYS** AFTER THE F.B.I. SUBPOENAED HIS WHITE-WATER FILES AND TAPES?

7-16

WHO ELSE WOULD BREAK THE STORY OF CHELSEA'S 7TH GRADE PAPER, "WHY I FEEL GUILTY BEING WHITE," THE **SAME DAY** CONGRESS VOTED AGAINST THE GULF WAR TO KEEP BUSH FROM BEING DEFEATED IN 1990?

NO **WONDER** I SCARE THEM!

HEY, KIDS! CAN **YOU** SPOT RUSH'S **BIG** LIES! THERE ARE **TEN** IN ALL!

IT'S EASY... **AND** EDU-CATIONAL! **HAVE FUN!**

INTRODUCTION

Amid the media furor that greeted the release of FAIR's June 1994 report, "Rush Limbaugh's Reign of Error," we received a call from a gentleman in western Massachusetts, who described himself as a Republican in his sixties. He had read news accounts of our report and wanted to get a copy . . . fast. In fact, he needed two copies, one for his son, one for his daughter—both "dittoheads," as Limbaugh fans call themselves.

"I just can't convince them that this guy is a phony, a four-flusher," the caller told us. "I'm retired. I can't get medical insurance. And Limbaugh claims every day we don't need to do anything about health care."

The man's call was like so many we received—people seeking the report for friends, relatives, or coworkers who they felt had been taken in by Limbaugh. Some wanted simply to give the report to the Limbaugh diehards they knew; others wanted to read it themselves as preparation for ongoing debates with the dittoheads in their lives. Some spoke of loved ones who had become dittoheads as if these people had run off and joined a fanatical cult.

The extraordinary demand for our original nine-page report is what prompted us to produce this book. Some readers may want to use the book as some sort of "dittohead deprogrammer."

But as a media watch group, FAIR (Fairness & Accuracy In Reporting) published the original report primarily as a wake-up call to mainstream media. How is it, we asked, that so many journalists had given so little scrutiny to a man who is probably the most influential commentator in the country? With daily broadcasts on more than 650 radio and 250 TV stations heard by over

"I do not lie on this program. And I do not make things up for the advancement of my cause. And if I find that I have been mistaken or am in error then I proclaim it generally at the top of—beginning of—a program, or as loudly as I can."—Rush Limbaugh (Radio show, 8/30/93)

"Most of us here in the media are what I consider infotainers. . . . Rush Limbaugh is what I call a disinfotainer. He entertains by spreading disinformation."—Comedian Al Franken at the White House Correspondents' Dinner (4/23/94)

20 million people every week, Limbaugh is among the most powerful political broadcasters in our country's history.

Sure, mainstream pundits had bickered over how much clout Limbaugh wields, or whether he's too mean-spirited, or whether he's "more entertainer than commentator." But few journalists had ever looked at more basic questions: Does he get his facts right? Does he tell the truth? Does he make things up?

Our report—coupled with the total inability of Limbaugh and his defenders to document or support any of his wild assertions (see Afterword)—is what finally pushed the accuracy question into the center of the national debate over Limbaugh. This book aims to deepen that debate.

Contrary to Limbaugh's protestations, this work offers ample evidence that the self-described "truth detector" does lie and does make things up to advance his cause. Indeed, many of his "truths" would be laughable if not for the millions of people who believe them. Here are just some of the claims that we decode and debunk in the pages that follow:

- "Even if polar ice caps melted, there would be no rise in ocean levels";
- "There are more acres of forest land in America today than when Columbus discovered the continent in 1492";
- "The poorest people in America are better off than the mainstream families of Europe";
- "The videotape of the Rodney King beating played absolutely no role in the conviction" of the police officers;
- "No one ever accuses Louis Farrakhan of being anti-Semitic";
- "There is a law coming down . . . which says that if you have a Bible at your desk at work, then you are guilty of religious harassment";

- The Clintons send their daughter to a school in which eighth-graders must write a paper: "Why I Feel Guilty Being White";

- "Most Canadian physicians" come to the United States when in need of surgery;
- Journalists in the 1992 presidential debates "didn't dare ask about foreign policy";
- "There is not one indictment" from Lawrence Walsh's Iran-Contra investigation.

UNCHALLENGED DEMAGOGUERY

From ozone to abortion, from Rodney King to Reaganomics, from Hillary Clinton to the homeless, Rush Limbaugh has a finely honed ability to twist and distort reality. Yet his facts are almost never challenged on his programs. Despite Limbaugh's claims to the contrary, hostile callers don't often get through the screeners on his radio show. His TV show is just him doing a sit-down monologue in front of a cheering audience. Transcripts of his TV program look at first glance like a typical script—until you notice that on page after page, every speaker is LIMBAUGH, LIMBAUGH, LIMBAUGH, with the monologue punctuated only by "Laughter" or "Applause." No one in the history of national television has had such a partisan—and uncontested—political platform.

Only on rare occasions does Limbaugh correct a mistake. If he retracted all his errors, the corrections would take up a sizeable portion of the program. One of Limbaugh's few apologies was made in 1992 to the aerosol industry for implying that spray cans still had CFCs in them. (CFCs were banned by Congress in 1978.) Another time, he apologized to Ted Koppel because his book jacket had mistakenly labeled Koppel a "liberal."

Limbaugh's chronic inaccuracy, and his lack of accountability, wouldn't be such a problem if he were just an obnoxious entertainer, like Howard Stern. But Limbaugh is taken seriously by "serious" media: In addition to repeat "Nightline" appearances, he's been an "expert" on such chat shows as "Today," "MacNeil/Lehrer NewsHour," "Charlie Rose," and "This Week with David Brinkley." The *New York Times, Los Angeles Times,* and *Newsweek* have published his columns.

Big-name journalists have actually lauded his grasp of facts. Ted Koppel, an unabashed fan of Limbaugh's radio show, says of the talkshow host (*American Spectator,* 9/92): "He's very smart. He does his homework. He is well-informed." A *U.S. News & World Report* piece (8/16/93) by Steven Roberts declared, "The information Mr. Limbaugh provides is generally accurate." Tim Russert, NBC's Washington bureau chief who hosted Limbaugh on "Meet the Press," was quoted about Limbaugh: "You have to give him credit—he works hard at getting his facts right." *(Rush to Us)*

Limbaugh is also taken seriously as a political figure. Supreme Court Justice Clarence Thomas, who officiated at Limbaugh's 1994 wedding, says he tapes Limbaugh's radio show so he can listen to it when he exercises (*USA Today,* 5/13/94). A cover story in the conservative *National Review* (9/6/93) declared Limbaugh "the leader of the opposition." Ronald Reagan called him "the number one voice for conservatism in our country." Columnist George Will referred to him as "the fourth branch of government." Former Secretary of Education William Bennett went beyond politics, describing Limbaugh as "possibly our greatest living American." (*American Spectator,* 9/92)

LOST IN THE OZONE: A CASE STUDY

If there's a method to Limbaugh's madness, it is to seize upon a theme and pound away on it day after day, as if through sheer force of repetition, a wild theory could somehow be transmuted into a factually based doctrine. To achieve his sleight of hand, Limbaugh will sometimes make allusions to vaguely identified sources or experts who purportedly back him up. To those intent on believing him or lacking the time to research and critically analyze what he's preaching, Limbaugh can appear to be developing his theories from the facts. In reality, he tends to concoct his facts to fit his theories. His ozone theory provides a case study.

Limbaugh has gotten a lot of mileage out of his contention that volcanoes do more harm to the ozone layer than human-produced chemicals do. He featured it in his best-selling book, *The Way Things Ought to Be* (paperback edition, pp. 155–157): "Mount Pinatubo in the Philippines spewed forth more than a thousand times the amount of ozone-depleting chemicals in one eruption than all the fluorocarbons manufactured by wicked, diabolical, and insensitive corporations in history. . . . Mankind can't possibly equal the output of even one eruption from Pinatubo, much less 4 billion years' worth of them, so how can we destroy ozone?"

Limbaugh calls concern about the ozone layer "balderdash" and "poppycock." The only people who worry about it are "environmental wackos" or "dunderheaded alarmists and prophets of doom."

Syndicated columnist Thomas Sowell used the volcano theory (*New York Post*, 1/14/94) as Exhibit A to illustrate Limbaugh's "very well-informed and savvy understanding of the political issues of our time." Sowell wrote: "While far more pretentious people have been joining the chorus of hysteria over 'global warming,' Limbaugh pointed out in his [first] book that one of the high readings of greenhouse gases in the atmosphere came right after a volcanic eruption—and volcanoes can put more gases into the atmosphere than the entire human race."

The alert reader will notice that Sowell has mixed up global warming and the ozone layer, two different issues. Still, Sowell concluded of Limbaugh, "It is obvious that the man has done his homework—and done it well."

Ted Koppel must have thought so, too, when he invited Limbaugh to be on "Nightline" (2/4/92) as an environmental "expert," opposite then Senator Al Gore. "If you listen to what Senator Gore said," Limbaugh proclaimed, "it is man-made products which are causing the ozone depletion, yet Mount Pinatubo has put 570 times the amount of chlorine into the atmosphere in one eruption than all of man-made chlorofluorocarbons [CFCs] in one year."

On his radio show, his syndicated TV show, and in two best-selling books, Limbaugh has advanced the idea that volcanoes are the real ozone culprits. This theory, like so many of Limbaugh's claims, has only one problem: Limbaugh doesn't know what he's talking about.

ERUPTION OF DISTORTION

"Chlorine from natural sources is soluble, and so it gets rained out of the lower atmosphere," the journal *Science* explained (6/11/93). "CFCs, in contrast, are insoluble and inert and thus make it to the stratosphere to release their chlorine." *Science* also noted that chlorine found in the stratosphere—where it can eat away at Earth's protective ozone layer—is always found with other by-products of CFCs, and not with the by-products of natural chlorine sources.

"Ozone depletion is real, as certain as Neil Armstrong's landing on the moon," Dr. Sherwood Rowland, an atmospheric chemist at the University of California at Irvine and an officer of the National Academy of Sciences, told us. "Natural causes of ozone depletion are not significant."

But Limbaugh didn't rely on atmospheric scientists for his information about the ozone layer: He dismissed them as members of the "agenda-oriented scientific community." Instead, he turned to Dixy Lee Ray, a former Washington State governor and Atomic Energy Commission chair, who wrote *Trashing the Planet*—"the most footnoted, documented book I have ever read," Limbaugh says.

If you check Ray's footnotes, you'll find that a main source for the volcano theory is Rogelio Maduro, the associate editor of *21st Century Science & Technology*. Maduro may not be part of the "scientific community" (though he does have a bachelor's degree in geology), but he certainly has an agenda: His magazine is produced by followers of cult leader Lyndon LaRouche, who believes that environmental protection is a genocidal plot masterminded by the queen of England and other sinister forces.

The volcano theorists can't even keep their stories straight. In his book, Limbaugh writes that the 1991 Pinatubo eruption put 1,000 times more chlorine into the atmosphere than industry has *ever* produced through CFCs; yet on "Nightline," Pinatubo is alleged to have produced 570 times the equivalent of *one year's worth* of CFCs. Both can't be right. It turns out neither is.

The figure 570 apparently derives from Ray's book—but she said it was Mount Augustine, an Alaskan volcano that erupted in 1976, which put out 570 times as much chlorine as one year's worth of CFCs. Ray's source seems to be a 1980 *Science* magazine article—but that piece was actually talking about the chlorine produced by a gigantic eruption that occurred 700,000 years ago in California. (*Science*, 6/11/93)

As our book shows, this kind of sloppiness, ignorance, and/or fabrication is run-of-the-mill in Limbaugh's commentary.

"Limbaugh quotes Dixy Lee Ray, who was wrong on nearly everything, did no research, took no part in academy debates, just made point-of-view pronouncements from right field. You can find someone with a Ph.D. to say something about anything. It makes it hard for the media to know whom to trust; that's why there's a National Research Council of the National Academy of Sciences, to allow people who really work on these projects to debate and assess. Limbaugh's sources are rarely in these assessment groups. But the media give someone like Limbaugh equal time with the

"We have too many people in this country," says Limbaugh, "who don't care about the integrity, character, honesty of their leaders." Shouldn't we also care about the honesty and integrity of a "leader" heard by more than 20 million people a week?

In this book, we compile some of Limbaugh's more obvious whoppers in order to persuade journalists, political leaders, and the public that when Limbaugh says, "I'm not making this up, folks," it's time to plug in your lie detector. When a college professor called Limbaugh's broadcast production company to check some of the talkshow host's "irrefutable evidence," he couldn't find anyone at the multi-million-dollar operation charged with researching or fact checking what Limbaugh says.

Journalists, in particular, have an obligation to challenge Limbaugh's brand of hysteria. Someone who has amassed a powerful political following through the regular use of half-truth and distortion is begging for tough media scrutiny. In 1954, Edward R. Murrow confronted Senator Joe McCarthy, another demagogue who had a similar allergy to facts and documentation. Today's TV networks ask themselves not how they can challenge Limbaugh's reign of error, but how they can profit from him. CBS News, the platform from which Murrow exposed McCarthy, tried to hire Limbaugh as a political commentator in 1994.

Real democracy is built on debate. But Limbaugh has little use for debates; he has forged a media empire largely on unchallenged monologues. "As he was fond of saying," wrote biographer Paul Colford, "he did not field calls to his show in order to give vent to public sentiment, but rather to make himself look good." Limbaugh told the talk-radio trade magazine *Talkers:* "I never debate. That's not what I do."

Fellow right-wing talkshow host G. Gordon Liddy once declared that liberals "won't go on [Limbaugh's] program and go head-to-head with him." (*Washington Times,* 8/30/93) The truth is that Limbaugh doesn't invite opposing guests. And when Limbaugh was invited to respond to FAIR on neutral turf such as CNN or National Public Radio, he steadfastly refused to debate—even to defend his own veracity.

The following confrontation—Limbaugh vs. Reality—is an attempt at stimulating (or, at least, simulating) a debate.

The list of fallacies compiled here is hardly exhaustive. Limbaugh makes significant new errors of fact and restates old myths on broadcast after broadcast, in writing after writing. We believe that point is made in this short book of over 100 distortions; we could easily have compiled a list of 1,000 false claims—but the result would have been a monotonous, interminable tome. As journalist Joshua Shenk showed in two brief articles for the *New Republic* ("Limbaugh's Lies," 5/23/94; "Limbaugh's Lies II," 8/8/94), scrutinizing the TV show for even a month or so results in errors too numerous to count.

We've assembled this Limbaugh comedy of errors from easily available sources—his two books, *The Way Things Ought to Be* and *See, I Told You So;* back issues of his glossy newsletter, the *Limbaugh Letter;* transcripts of ten months' worth of his TV show; gleanings from as much of his radio show as we could take; and other published evaluations of Limbaugh's accuracy. One publication, the *Flush Rush Quarterly* (*FRQ*), is largely devoted to chronicling Limbaugh's falsehoods.

Readers of this book may wonder whether some of these Limbaughisms are yanked out of context. But our problem was not cutting away context to make Limbaugh look worse or wackier than he is; the problem usually was deciding where to end a Limbaugh quote so we could focus on one or two errors and resist the temptation to point out yet more mistakes in the next few sen-

National Academy of Sciences. While the Academy represents the careful wisdom of scientists, Limbaugh and his ilk shoot from the hip, from a minority view hyping special interests. No responsible scientist says that every detail is solved, so it's easy to grab a caveat and turn it into a 'there's no problem here' and then get equal time on 'Nightline' with the scientific consensus view."
— Dr. Stephen Schneider, Stanford University climatologist and senior scientist at the National Center for Atmospheric Research, Boulder, Colorado

tences. After FAIR's original report was published, Limbaugh could not identify a single inaccurate or out-of-context quote.

In collecting these statements, we also took into account Limbaugh's sometimes twisted sense of humor. Some of the more ridiculous claims—those it's hard to believe anyone could take seriously—are included only because Limbaugh insisted that his audience should accept them as facts.

When he accuses Bill Clinton of being unable to tell the truth, Rush Limbaugh is fond of saying, "There's a pathology here, folks." It's a pathology Limbaugh knows firsthand.

1. Make-Believe Environment

LIMBAUGH: On global warming: "Even if polar ice caps melted, there would be no rise in ocean levels. . . . After all, if you have a glass of water with ice cubes in it, as the ice melts, it simply turns to liquid and the water level in the glass remains the same." (Radio, 6/19/92)

REALITY: Limbaugh's all wet. Most of the ice in the world is on land, in Antarctica. If that ice cap melted, sea level around the world would rise about 200 feet, producing catastrophic results. (Dr. Donald Blankenship, University of Texas Institute for Geophysics, *New York Times*, 2/23/93)

LIMBAUGH: "A Gallup poll of scientists involved in global climate research shows that 53 percent do not believe that global warming has occurred, 30 percent say they don't know, and only 17 percent are devotees of this dubious theory." (*Told You So*, p. 162)

REALITY: These numbers totally distort the Gallup poll (released 2/92), which found that the overwhelming majority of scientists surveyed—66 percent—believed that human-induced global warming has occurred. Only 10 percent disagreed, and the rest were undecided. Without doing any fact checking, Limbaugh apparently lifted his faulty figures from a George Will column (*Washington Post,* 9/3/92) or from the *National Review* article (9/14/92) that had prompted Will's error. Limbaugh recirculated the bogus poll numbers even after Gallup had taken the unusual step of issuing a written statement correcting Will: "Most scientists involved in research in this area do believe human-induced global warming is occurring now." (*San Francisco Chronicle,* 9/27/92)

APPARENTLY THESE ACTIVISTS WOULD RATHER RISK THE HEALTH OF EVERY LIVING BEING ON THE PLANET THAN ADMIT THE *POSSIBILITY* OF A PROBLEM...RUSH LIMBAUGH LEADS THE CHARGE, VOCIFEROUSLY DENYING THE VERY *EXISTENCE* OF A HOLE IN THE OZONE...

HEY--ALL THOSE SCIENTISTS HAVE ARE A BUNCH OF INSTRUMENTS AND MEASUREMENTS!

I HAVE AN IDEOLOGY!

EIB
EXTREMISM IN BROADCASTING

LIMBAUGH: "There are more acres of forest land in America today than when Columbus discovered the continent in 1492." (*Told You So,* p. 171) "Do you know we have more acreage of forest land in the United States today than we did at the time the Constitution was written?" (Radio, 2/18/94)

REALITY: The forest land before European settlement in what are now the 50 states covered about 1 billion acres, according to U.S. Forest Service historian Douglas MacCleery. *(American Forests)* The vast majority of this forest still stood at the end of the eighteenth century—roughly 930 million acres. *(Encyclopedia of American Forest and Conservation History)* Today, there are only 737 million acres of forest land, much of which lacks the ecological diversity of the original old-growth forest. *(American Forests)*

"Limbaugh's environmental opinions have more in common with science fiction than with science fact."
—Michael Oppenheimer, senior scientist, Environmental Defense Fund

LIMBAUGH: On regulations placed on charcoal lighter fluid in the L.A. area: "Do you know what charcoal lighter fluid is? Ninety-five percent of the contents of charcoal lighter fluid are kerosene. Ninety-five percent of jet fuel is kerosene. Now, my friends, does it not stand to reason—this is where I get the logic of reasoning once again, does it not stand to reason that [given] the traffic at LAX and John Wayne Airport in Orange County—the amount of kerosene needed to propel a Boeing 747 into the air is probably more than all the kerosene used by outdoor barbecue fanatics in a day?" (Radio, Fall 1990)

REALITY: Kerosene is not used in charcoal lighter fluid, say manufacturers of the two dominant brands, Kingsford and Wizard. A Southern California pollution board restricted lighter fluids in October 1990 because they contained high levels of volatile hydrocarbons that contribute to the formation of ground-level ozone, a health hazard. When airplanes burn jet fuel (which *is* a form of kerosene), they produce mainly carbon dioxide and water vapor, which do not contribute to ozone.

LIMBAUGH: Responding to an environmentalist's call for a ban on throwaway Styrofoam packaging, Limbaugh declared: "Styrofoam and plastic milk jugs are biodegradable! Do you know what isn't biodegradable? Paper!" (Radio, 6/15/91) A week later, when listener Michael Corman sent Limbaugh a letter refuting this claim, Limbaugh derided the letter on the air: "I never said that Styrofoam is biodegradable." Weeks after that, when Corman managed to get on the air, Limbaugh moved back to his earlier claim: "Well, it doesn't happen in a lifetime, Mike, that's the trouble with you enviro-Nazis, you want everything to happen in your lifetime! You can't live for 2,000 years to see if it might degrade. We don't know. Nobody does. It hasn't been tested."

REALITY: The biodegradability of polystyrene (commonly called Styrofoam) *has* been tested. It's a "virtually indestructible non-biodegradable plastic," according to *Chemical Marketing Reporter* (2/12/90). Paper, by contrast, is made of cellulose, which can be digested by bacteria under proper conditions.

"On no issue has the evidence of my foresight and keen political instincts been more compelling than that of the environment." (**Told You So**, *p. 171*)

LIMBAUGH: "We closed down a whole town—Times Beach, Missouri—over the threat of dioxin. We now know there was no reason to do that. Dioxin at those levels isn't harmful." (*Ought to Be*, p. 163)

REALITY: The year before Limbaugh's book was released, the *New England Journal of Medicine* (1/24/91) published a new study on dioxin exposure and cancer, declaring, "The hypothesis that low exposures are entirely safe for humans is distinctly less tenable now than before." Subsequent studies have reaffirmed dioxin's deadly effects; a September 1994 EPA report confirmed that dioxin causes cancer, and suggested that even trace amounts may be a risk to immune, reproductive, and developmental systems. (*AP*, 9/13/94)

LIMBAUGH: "There are two types of asbestos: One is potentially lethal and one is as harmless as a Cheez Doodle. . . . The Cheez Doodle variety of asbestos is known as chrysotile. It accounts for 95 percent of the asbestos used in the United States. And it is utterly, totally harmless." (TV, 9/20/93)

On Actors Who Support Environmentalism:

"As actors, they're good at fooling people. They're good at convincing you they're something they're not, including being an expert." (TV, Earth Day 1993)

 LIMBAUGH: "On April 23, 1994, a woman named Barbara Schoener, 40 years old, was killed by an 82-pound mountain lion in El Dorado County, California. . . . She has two kids and a husband. The collection fund had been started for a trust fund for the kids and their education, but at the same time a companion fund had been started by a bunch of animal rights activists for the orphaned lion cubs. . . . As of May 23, the orphaned mountain lion had received $21,000 in donations and Barbara Schoener's two kids had received around $9,000." (TV, 7/5/94)

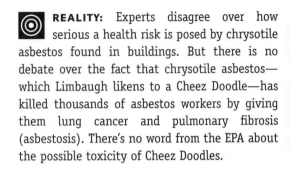 **REALITY:** Experts disagree over how serious a health risk is posed by chrysotile asbestos found in buildings. But there is no debate over the fact that chrysotile asbestos—which Limbaugh likens to a Cheez Doodle—has killed thousands of asbestos workers by giving them lung cancer and pulmonary fibrosis (asbestosis). There's no word from the EPA about the possible toxicity of Cheez Doodles.

On Actors Who Oppose Environmentalism:

Ronald Reagan is "my hero. The best president in my lifetime."

 REALITY: On May 31, Folsom City Zoo official Terry Jenkins sent a letter to Limbaugh correcting an earlier broadcast: "There has never been a 'trust fund for the kitten' as you reported, nor any other fund-raising efforts by the zoo or anyone else (with the exception of $36 raised by the coffee store across the street). There certainly have not been any 'animal rights people' deciding to set one up as you claim they have." ABC's "20/20" debunked the story on June 4, with Barbara Walters concluding: "Unsolicited public donations have come in for the cub, but so far they total less than $3,000, so people do care more about children than cubs." A month later, Limbaugh was still sticking with his distorted version.

THE GREAT PRETENDER

Rush Limbaugh has made a career attacking vegetarians, animal rights activists, and environmentalists. They are the ne'er-do-well extremists who tear down achievers like him. Yet for the opening of every Limbaugh radio show, he lifts the instrumental portion of the Pretenders' rock song "My City Was Gone"—a song expressing sharp environmentalist sentiments. One verse goes: *"I went back to Ohio, but my pretty countryside/ Had been paved down the middle by a government that had no pride/ The farms of Ohio had been replaced by shopping malls/ And Muzak filled the air from Seneca to Cuyahoga Falls."* The words and music were written by Pretenders' lead singer Chrissie Hynde—a vegetarian, pro-animal rights, leftish unwed mother.

2. Bogus Economics

LIMBAUGH: "The poorest people in America are better off than the mainstream families of Europe." (Radio; *FRQ,* Spring/93)

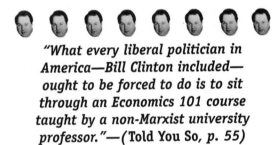

"What every liberal politician in America—Bill Clinton included—ought to be forced to do is to sit through an Economics 101 course taught by a non-Marxist university professor."—(**Told You So,** *p. 55*)

REALITY: The poorest 20 percent of Americans can purchase an average of $5,433 worth of goods with their income, according to World Bank figures published in *World Development Report 1994*. Meanwhile, in Germany, the average person can purchase $20,610 worth of goods; in France, $19,200; in Britain, $16,730. America's poor are not even better off than average citizens in many Eastern European nations, like the Czech Republic ($7,160), Russia ($6,220), and Hungary ($5,740). Not only are the U.S. poor nowhere close to mainstream living standards in most of Europe, they are worse off than the poor in many European countries—like Germany, Sweden, and Holland. (The World Bank uses a measure called "Purchasing Power Parity" to compare living standards—a method Limbaugh endorsed in the *Limbaugh Letter,* 1/94.)

LIMBAUGH: "Kansas City per capita now has more people working for government than they have working in the private sector, so it's a perfect place for the president to go. That's—it's a true story. Now when you combine the city, state, federal, and all—more people work for government there than work in the private sector." (TV, 6/15/94)

REALITY: In the Kansas City metropolitan area, 45,000 out of approximately 850,000 workers are employed by the federal, state, and local governments—about 5 percent of total workers. (*The New Republic,* 8/8/94)

LIMBAUGH: On California contractor C. C. Myers completing repairs 74 days early on the earthquake-damaged Santa Monica Freeway: "There was one key element that made this happen. One key thing: The governor of California declared [it] a disaster area and by so doing eliminated the need for competitive bids." (TV, 4/13/94) "They gave this guy [Myers] the job without having to go through the rigmarole . . . of giving 25 percent of the job to a minority-owned business and 25 percent to a woman. . . . All those federal rules got suspended. . . . Government got the hell out of the way." (TV, 4/15/94)

REALITY: There was competitive bidding. Myers beat four other contractors for the job. Affirmative action rules did apply. At least 40 percent of the subcontracts went to minority or women-owned firms. Far from getting out of the way, dozens of state employees were on the job 24 hours a day. Furthermore, the federal government picked up the tab for the whole job. (*Los Angeles Times*, 5/1/94)

LIMBAUGH: "Banks take the risks in issuing student loans and they are entitled to the profits." (Radio; *FRQ*, Summer/93)

REALITY: Banks take no risks in issuing student loans, which are federally insured.

LIMBAUGH: "Al Gore was in the [1992] debates running around trying to say that the Bush administration was sending representatives to corporate boardrooms, knocking on the door and saying, 'Hey, you know what, if you guys close up and put a bunch of Americans out of work, and relocate in Mexico, we'll give you some tax benefits.' It's not happening. That kind of thing isn't happening." (Radio, 8/19/93)

REALITY: Gore charged that the Bush administration had "subsidized the moving of U.S. factories to foreign countries." He was referring to the Private Sector Program of the U.S. Agency for International Development, which did indeed subsidize low-wage "free economic zones" in Central America and the Caribbean, to which U.S. manufacturing jobs were exported, as documented by "60 Minutes" (9/27/92), "Nightline" (9/29/92), and the National Labor Committee Education Fund.

LIMBAUGH: In praise of NAFTA: "I've got here the January–February issue of *Ford World,* employee newsletter—not written by management. Read along with me: 'Ford will create the equivalent of 1,000 jobs in the United States and Canada and will reactivate 300 jobs in Mexico by increasing exports to Mexico. . . . Vehicle exports to Mexico are expected to reach more than 50,000 a year by 1996.' So you AFL-CIO guys and Mr. Perot and you Perotistas, has this finally convinced you?" (TV, 2/23/94)

REALITY: *Ford World* is a company publication, we were told by a *Ford World* spokesperson. It is run by Ford management and gives management's views. What *Ford World* doesn't emphasize is that while Ford hopes to export 50,000 cars yearly to Mexico (from the United States and Canada), a new $60 million investment in Mexican factories will ensure that about 85,000 cars are built there and imported each year to the United States (*Automotive News,* 10/3/94). AFL-CIO guys won't easily be convinced by a company organ being camouflaged as an "employee newsletter."

L I M B A U G H   V E R S U S   L I M B A U G H

"We are, quite bluntly, broke. We don't have the money to sustain the dreams and experiments of liberalism any longer. We have a $400 billion a year budget deficit and a $4 trillion debt." (*Ought to Be,* p. 308)

"That means our debt—yearly debt—is only 2.9 percent of our total budget. If you at home could say that the total amount of your debt was only 2.9 percent of all that you earn and produce, you'd be happy. This deficit is a straw dog. It's always been a phony monster. This is manageable debt as long as our economy stays strong." (TV, 7/8/94)

A SPIN DOCTORATE IN REAGANOMICS

LIMBAUGH: "Don't let the liberals deceive you into believing that a decade of sustained growth without inflation in America [in the '80s] resulted in a bigger gap between the haves and the have-nots. Figures compiled by the Congressional Budget Office dispel that myth." (*Ought to Be,* p. 70)

REALITY: CBO numbers for after-tax incomes show that in 1980, the richest fifth of our country had eight times the income of the poorest fifth. By 1989, the ratio was more than twenty to one.

LIMBAUGH: On news reports that Bill Clinton's budget deficit might drop to $180 billion: "$180 billion is still billions more than any of the eeevil deficits Reagan ever ran up." (*Limbaugh Letter,* 4/94)

REALITY: Eeerroneous. Reagan's budget deficits from 1983 through 1986 all exceeded $180 billion dollars, with the 1986 deficit over $220 billion. (Adjusting for inflation to 1994 dollars, all eight Reagan deficits were over $180 billion.)

LIMBAUGH: "Oh, how they relished blaming Reagan administration policies, including the mythical reductions in HUD's budget for public housing, for creating all of the homeless! Budget cuts? There were no budget cuts! The budget figures show that actual construction of public housing *increased* during the Reagan years." (*Ought to Be,* pp. 242–243)

REALITY: In 1980, there were 20,900 low-income public housing units under construction; in 1988, there were 9,700, a decline of 54 percent (*Statistical Abstract of the U.S.*). The HUD budget for the construction of new public housing was slashed from $3.7 billion in 1980 to $573 million in 1988. "We're getting out of the housing business. Period," a Reagan HUD official declared in 1985. (Low Income Housing Information Service; *The Housing Part of The Homeless Problem* by Chester Hartman)

LIMBAUGH: "Ronald Reagan cut everything in the budget, and yet they say he made the biggest deficit in the country. I don't know how they come up with that. It's Washington math." (Radio; *Flush Rush,* a book by Brian Keliher)

REALITY: Reagan didn't cut the military budget; it reached historic highs under the man Limbaugh calls "Ronaldus Maximus"—as did our country's national debt and deficits. (*Budget of the U.S. Government, 1995*—Historical Tables)

LIMBAUGH: On Barbra Streisand: "Now this is a woman who decries the '80s as a decade of greed and selfishness, yet during the '80s she signed a $60 million recording contract with Sony, which bought Columbia." (TV, 3/24/94)

REALITY: It wasn't during the '80s that Streisand signed the contract with Sony—it was December 1992. The contract involved records and movies. (*Washington Post,* 12/16/92)

LIMBAUGH: Complaining about critics of Reaganomics: "Reagan has been out of the White House for eight years." (Radio, 5/23/94)

REALITY: He'd been out less than five and a half years.

RUSH LIMBAUGH, TAX COUNSELOR

A newly trained tax preparer at H & R Block earns a few hundred dollars per week. Although Limbaugh earns a few hundred thousand dollars per week, the information he dispenses about taxes isn't worth a dollar.

LIMBAUGH: Railing against Clinton's retroactive income tax hike: "How many of you people in the audience think that you weren't going to have a tax increase? It was only going to be the rich that were going to have a tax increase and you weren't." (TV, 5/17/93)

REALITY: The retroactive tax increase applied only to individuals with taxable incomes over $115,000 a year, or couples with taxable incomes over $140,000 a year—the richest 1.2 percent of the United States population.

LIMBAUGH: "You better pay attention to the 1993 budget deal because there is an increase in beer and alcohol taxes." (Radio, 7/9/93)

REALITY: The 1993 budget deal contained no increase in beer and alcohol taxes—either in its final version or the versions that had passed the House and Senate at the time Limbaugh made this remark.

LIMBAUGH: "Let me tell you about imputed income. Let's say you own a home and you live in it, but you could, if you wanted to, rent it for, say, $200 a month. Two hundred times 12 is $2,400. Under Bill Clinton you will have to add $2,400 to your total income because that's the imputed value of your asset and then pay taxes on it. Not making this up." (TV, 2/25/93)

REALITY: He certainly was. Although imputed income has long been used to determine economic statistics, no one has ever had to pay taxes on it, and Clinton never proposed that anyone should.

LIMBAUGH: "Somebody show me where in history giving tax breaks made somebody wealthy." (Radio, 7/27/93)

REALITY: That day's *Los Angeles Times* featured a front-page article headlined "Developers Get $366 Million Tax Break in Budget Bill." It reported that fiscal austerity had not stopped Washington politicians "from finding a few hundred million dollars for politically influential real estate developers." Tax breaks have made many somebodies wealthy in such industries as oil, banking, utilities, insurance, and agribusiness.

RUSH LIMBAUGH: CHAMPION OF THE OVERDOG

Who says Rush Limbaugh is abusive to minorities? He champions various minority interests: multimillionaires, bankers, owners of private planes and yachts, drug companies, the tobacco industry. It's only those other "minorities"—women, workers, union members, the poor, racial minorities, immigrants, gays—for whom he has little compassion.

"One of the things I want to do before I die is conduct the homeless Olympics. . . . [Events would include] the 10-Meter Shopping Cart Relay, the Dumpster Dig, and the Hop, Skip, and Trip." (*Los Angeles Times,* 1/20/91)

On a *New York Times* ad bought by clergy members who likened inadequate support for homeless people to denying Mary and Joseph a room at the inn: "What unmitigated gall! Imagine comparing the Virgin Mary and Joseph, a gainfully employed carpenter, with some street people." (*Ought to Be,* p. 246)

On an artist's work, "The Homeless Trap," that employed a large mousetraplike device and used a bedroll as bait: "I've got this idea. Instead of one of these, have a thousand of them. And use them as a solution—not as a piece of art. Just put these things all over the city and if they trap homeless people, use them." (TV, 3/9/94)

On NAFTA: "If we are going to start rewarding no skills and stupid people—I'm serious, let the unskilled jobs, let the kinds of jobs that take absolutely no knowledge whatsoever to do—let stupid and unskilled Mexicans do that work." (Radio; *FRQ,* Fall/93)

"This is asinine! A Cesar Chavez Day in California? Wasn't he convicted of a crime?" (Radio; *FRQ*, Winter/94)

"I don't give a hoot that [Columbus] gave some Indians a disease that they didn't have immunity against." (*Ought to Be*, p. 45)

On the endangered Northern Spotted Owl: "If the owl can't adapt to the superiority of humans, screw it." (*Ought to Be*, p. 162)

"Kurt Cobain was, ladies and gentleman, a worthless shred of human debris." (TV, 4/11/94)

"Those of you who want to take off the Clinton/Gore bumper stickers, just go get a handicapped parking sticker instead, and people will know why you voted that way." (Radio, 7/23/93)

"Militant feminists are pro-choice because it's their ultimate avenue of power over men. . . . It is their attempt to impose their will on the rest of society, particularly on men." (*Ought to Be*, p. 53)

"Why is it that whenever a corporation fires workers it is never speculated that the workers might have deserved it?" (*Ought to Be*, p. 275)

"If you choose to believe this class warfare propaganda that the S&L was nothing but a bailout for the rich, think about this. Who invested in the S&Ls? You. Individual people. . . . If you're tired of bailing out the S&Ls, then send back the money that you've got." (*Flush Rush*)

"How many of you can remember—honestly—hearing your friends, your neighbors, or strangers complaining and moaning about health insurance on a general basis?" (TV, 7/14/94; *With an estimated $18 million income in '94, Limbaugh needn't moan about health insurance.*)

THE MAN AND THE MYTH

How did Limbaugh get to this pinnacle of power? Don't look to Limbaugh for the answers. He is no more accurate or dependable when discussing his favorite subject—himself—than he is when discussing the ozone layer or health care. He portrays his roots as typical American middle class, but that's an understatement. He was born into a well-to-do, well-connected Republican family of lawyers and bankers in Cape Girardeau, Missouri. His father was a corporate lawyer and Republican leader. His grandfather, Rush Limbaugh Sr., was a member of the Missouri House of Representatives and president of the Missouri bar association; his uncle was appointed to a federal judgeship by Ronald Reagan; a first cousin sits on the Missouri Supreme Court.

"Nobody handed it to me on a silver platter," Limbaugh once boasted about his broadcasting career. "I had to work at it to prove myself every step of the way." Not quite. He got his first job hosting a radio show, at the age of 16, thanks to the fact that his dad was part-owner of the station. (*The Rush Limbaugh Story* by Paul Colford)

Limbaugh has made a career assailing Bill Clinton as a "draft dodger" whose evasiveness on the subject proves that he has a "character flaw." But Limbaugh himself has been evasive about his own avoidance of the Vietnam draft. He's offered this account: "Upon taking a physical, [I] was discovered to have a physical—uh, by virtue of what the military says, I didn't even know it existed—a physical deferment, and then the lottery system came along . . . and mine [number] was high." On another occasion, he said that he had a "pilonidal cyst" and a "football knee from high school," and claimed: "I made no effort to evade it or avoid it."

Limbaugh's explanations, as biographer Colford has shown, are deceptive. Limbaugh never had a draft board physical. It was only after Limbaugh drew a lottery number that *kept him in the running* for the draft, records show, that Limbaugh himself provided medical information to the board of some minor problem that took him out of consideration for Vietnam. Limbaugh's dad had the same kind of pilonidal cyst, but served in World War II. No evidence has surfaced of a football injury. Limbaugh once joked on the air that maybe his dad bribed the draft board to keep him out of Vietnam.

A comparison of Limbaugh's life with his talk reveals some of the contradictions and hypocrisies that are the core of Limbaughism. He was a strong supporter of the Vietnam War, which he neatly avoided. He's a great patriot who didn't register to vote until he was 35 years old—after a columnist exposed his lack of civic duty. (Limbaugh hails Ronald Reagan as "the best president in my lifetime," but never bothered to vote for him.) He decries the high divorce rate—which he blames on liberals or the 1960s—while he's working on his third marriage. He is a crusader for God and religion, but does not attend church.

IN THE WILDERNESS

Limbaugh dropped out of college after a year to pursue his radio career. A break came in 1971 when he was hired as a Top 40 deejay in the Pittsburgh area (using the moniker Jeff Christie). But he was fired the next year, according to Limbaugh, "for playing 'Under My Thumb' by the Rolling Stones too many times." Says Limbaugh, "I loved the song . . . and I violated the music rotation by playing it every day."

Saluting the brave American soldiers of World War II: "Young men lied about their age, ignored medical and physical disqualifications, and abandoned their livelihoods in order to join the services." (Told You So, p. 253)

In 1983, the former journeyman deejay got a job as a radio newscaster at KMBZ in Kansas City, later becoming a commentator and then a talkshow host. He once interrupted his reading of news headlines to warn that he'd erupt in a rage at the next mention of Eleanor Roosevelt (thus foreshadowing his reaction to a future First Lady). His on-air shtick included remarks about what Geraldine Ferraro would do to the country every 28 days if she became president, and how Ted Kennedy would make a great leader of the Soviet Union. He was let go after 10 months.

But Limbaugh was not unemployed for long. A few weeks later, as fate would have it, a certain Morton Downey Jr. was fired

at Sacramento radio station KFBK over an ethnic slur; Limbaugh was called in to replace him. It was Limbaugh's four-year Sacramento stint that paved the way to his national show.

Ironically, the individual who helped save Limbaugh's career by championing and grooming him for the Sacramento job was radio executive Norm Woodruff; he died a few years later of AIDS—a gay man Limbaugh has never talked much about. In Sacramento, Limbaugh gained fame by making light of the AIDS crisis ("Rock Hudson's disease") and by launching his "Gerbil Update" segment, which was based on Limbaugh's charge that gays used the small rodents for sexual stimulation.

When Limbaugh declared the National Organization for Women "a terrorist organization," California NOW demanded a retraction—but was granted instead an interview on Limbaugh's show. He interviewed two women from NOW and let them make some points; after the women left the studio, he scoffed on-air at the two "ugly dogs."

Limbaugh's harangues sparked a local activist to try to place an ad in the city's leading daily, the *Sacramento Bee,* in hopes of rallying critics of the talkshow host. But the newspaper—owned by the McClatchy family, which also owned the station—refused to print the ad.

GOING NATIONAL

The key player in taking Limbaugh national in 1988 was Ed McLaughlin, who had retired as president of ABC Radio Networks two years earlier. Thanks to a deal with ABC, McLaughlin was able to pluck the unknown Limbaugh from Sacramento to New York—and get him instantly on the air in New York and some 60 or more other markets. ABC's sales staff sold the commercials for Limbaugh's national show. McLaughlin and Limbaugh became partners in the venture, although Limbaugh contributed no money. He enthused in his first book: "I knew, for the first time, what being a small businessman was really all about."

Thus was born Limbaugh's "Excellence In Broadcasting Network," which has one and only one show, his own. Hardly toned down after going national, he still referred to gays as "faggots" and "perverts." News items about AIDS were accompanied by Dionne Warwick's song, "I'll Never Love This Way Again." Feminists were "freaks" and "feminazis." Political opponents were still "commie-libs." Playing to conservative prejudices with jokes, hubris, and a demagogue's instinct for distortion—and operating beyond the critical scrutiny of mainstream journalism—his talkshow grew at an unprecedented rate.

By 1992, Limbaugh's carriage on 500 stations made him a powerful player in national politics. "My policy is: I don't involve myself in [Republican] primaries," Limbaugh proclaimed to *Playboy.* "After the party and people have chosen the candidate, then it's a different ball game."

This was certainly *not* Limbaugh's policy in 1992, when he

"When we come back, I'm going to ask both our guests if they think radio talkshows and especially Rush Limbaugh are a higher level of journalism than we've known before."—Pat Buchanan (CNN "Crossfire," 2/12/94)

supported Patrick Buchanan in the early primaries, urging listeners to back the right-wing challenger because George Bush had "let down people who elected him." If victorious, Buchanan pledged to appoint Limbaugh his White House communications director.

But Limbaugh would soon change horses and become a Bush booster. The courtship was nurtured by longtime Republican operative Roger Ailes, the Bush campaign's communications director in 1988 and the executive producer of Limbaugh's soon-to-be-launched TV show. Matchmaker Ailes arranged for Limbaugh to have a sleep-over date at the White House on June 3—which included dinner and seeing a musical with Bush.

"Despite Limbaugh's embarrassed protest," wrote reporter Paul Colford, "the president of the United States insisted on carrying his guest's overnight bag to the Lincoln Bedroom." From his room, "the wide-eyed guest" phoned his brother and then his mother: "You'll never guess where I am!" Colford wrote that "Limbaugh remained awake into the wee hours so that he could study and savor every detail of the Lincoln Bedroom." Virtually overnight, Limbaugh became a Bush backer.

With Roger Ailes behind the scenes, Limbaugh's nationally syndicated TV program, launched in September 1992, instantly became the most partisan national TV show in United States history. It offered program-long promos for Bush—and assaults on his opponents—that resembled half-hour campaign attack ads. All the while, Ailes was a high-level (though unpaid) adviser to the Bush campaign, and Limbaugh was receiving direct briefings from the campaign's political director, Mary Matalin. If Bush had to account for the worth of the Limbaugh broadcasts, his filing with the Federal Elections Commission might have exceeded legal limits by millions of dollars.

In January 1994, Limbaugh became the loudest partisan commentator on the Armed Forces Radio and Television Service

(AFRTS), which began airing the first hour of his radio talkshow each weekday. Portraying himself as a victim of censorship, Limbaugh used his TV and radio broadcasts to bully his way onto the network that serves military personnel and their families overseas—even though AFRTS surveys showed very little demand for Limbaugh. His occasional guest host, Representative Bob Dornan (R-CA), wrote a letter signed by 70 conservative Congress members accusing the "liberal leadership" of the Pentagon of muzzling Limbaugh.

When a Pentagon spokesperson suggested that adding Limbaugh would require "some sort of opposing view in our programming schedule," Limbaugh fumed that he was "livid" about "this balance business." (TV, 12/2/93) He would soon be added with *no* opposing program. Now United States troops across the globe can hear Limbaugh bemoan the fact that they have "this draft dodger as commander-in-chief."

3. Limbaugh's Law

Although he hails from a family of lawyers, he is no better informed on the law than he is on taxes.

 LIMBAUGH: "There's no such thing as an implied contract." (Radio; *FRQ,* Spring/93)

 REALITY: Every first-year law student knows there is. (*Corbin on Contracts*)

 LIMBAUGH: On why income taxes may be illegal: "There is actually an article in the Constitution prohibiting the transfer of funds from one individual to another." (Radio, 8/19/94)

REALITY: No there isn't. Income taxes were barred by constitutional clauses requiring taxes to be "apportioned" among the states "in proportion to the census." The Sixteenth Amendment, ratified in 1913, gave Congress the power to "collect taxes on income."

 LIMBAUGH: On the 1994 wedding of computer tycoon Bill Gates: "Bill Gates. Six billion dollars. He's got twice as much money as Perot. . . . He gets married. *Immediately* now he has three billion dollars." (Radio, 1/3/94; *The Rush Limbaugh Story*)

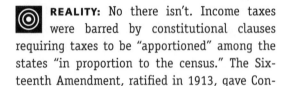 **REALITY:** When you marry, you don't get half your spouse's wealth. In states following community property rules (like Washington, where Gates resides), you're entitled in a divorce to half of the money your spouse earned *after* the marriage commenced—not half of the wealth he or she had already accumulated *before* the wedding.

LIMBAUGH   VERSUS LIMBAUGH

Rights of criminal defendants derided: "The way we approach the rights of accused criminals has changed so much over the past twenty-five years that if the same changes had taken place drastically, overnight, I am convinced the people wouldn't have put up with it. . . . With each ruling there is increasingly less concern for crime victims, victims' families, and potential victims." (*Ought to Be,* p. 170)

Later in the same book, rights of criminal defendants defended (in this case, those of the police officers in the Rodney King beating case): "The defendant is presumed innocent, the state has the burden of proof, the defendant's guilt must be proved beyond a reasonable doubt, etc. . . . Because our system accords special protection to the accused, the guilty sometimes go free in a close case, and that's the way the system was designed." (*Ought to Be,* p. 217)

4. Church and Mis-State

LIMBAUGH: "There is a law that's coming down, a regulation from the Equal Employment Opportunity Commission, which says that if you have a Bible at your desk at work, then you are guilty of religious harassment." (TV, 6/9/94)

REALITY: That very day, EEOC Executive Director Douglas Gallegos testified before a Senate subcommittee and declared that having a Bible on your desk is protected speech. (*The New Republic*, 8/8/94)

LIMBAUGH: "The Supreme Court has ordered that the Ten Commandments be removed from high school bulletin boards because they are based on religious teachings. That is in spite of the fact that it is the Ten Commandments that appear on the wall of the very room in which the Supreme Court meets." (*Ought to Be*, p. 279) "If you visit the U.S. Supreme Court building, you will see the Ten Commandments emblazoned on the wall right above the likenesses of the past justices." (*Told You So*, p. 85)

REALITY: The Supreme Court no more endorses the Ten Commandments than it does Confucianism. Decorations in the court chamber depict famous lawgivers from history—including Moses, Hammurabi, Solon, Draco, Confucius, and several others.

LIMBAUGH: "The First Amendment has been used to forcibly remove religion from not just our classrooms but all government institutions. . . . The way liberals are interpreting the First Amendment today is that it prevents anyone who is religious from being in government." (*Ought to Be*, p. 281)

REALITY: It didn't prevent Mormon bishop Orrin Hatch (R-UT) or ordained Episcopal priest John Danforth (R-MO) from being in the U.S. Senate. Or Rev. Ron Lewis (R-KY) or Rev. Floyd Flake (D-NY) from being in the U.S. House. It didn't prevent President Clinton from hiring Rev. William Gray, an ex-congressman, to help return former priest Jean-Bertrand Aristide to Haiti—with the help of Jimmy Carter, who taught Sunday school while he was president.

Limbaugh, Marilyn Quayle, Pat Robertson, Jerry Falwell; 1992 Republican National Convention

LIMBAUGH: "Ladies and gentlemen, we now know why there is this institutional opposition to low tax rates in the liberal wing of the Democratic Party. It's because [low tax rates] are biblical in nature and in root. When you can trace the lowering of tax rates on grain from 90 percent to 20 percent, giving seven fat years during the days of Pharaoh in Egypt, why then you are tracing the roots of lower taxes and rising prosperity to religion. . . . You can trace individual prosperity, economic growth back to the Bible, the Old Testament. Isn't it amazing?" (Radio, 6/28/93; *Told You So,* p. 72)

REALITY: Amazingly wrong. Genesis 41 is about the wisdom of *instituting* taxes, not cutting them. After Pharaoh had a dream that prophesied seven fat years to be followed by seven lean years, Joseph advised: "Pharaoh should take action and appoint supervisors over the land, and impose a tax of one-fifth on the land of Egypt during the seven years of plenty." (Genesis 41:34, *The Jerusalem Bible*) This 20 percent tax put grain aside for use during the famine, allowing Egypt to avoid hunger. The "90 percent" tax that Pharaoh supposedly cut is Limbaugh's own dream.

5. Civics 101

LIMBAUGH: "The Supreme Court has become the refuge of liberalism in our country, because liberalism has not found its way into our society legislatively." (TV, 11/2/92)

REALITY: At the time this statement was made, eight of the nine Supreme Court justices had been appointed by Republican presidents, four by Reagan. Republican appointees had held a majority on the Supreme Court for the previous 22 years.

LIMBAUGH: "Stop and think about this for a minute. Bill Clinton is the first president in modern history to have both houses of Congress. We've got every branch of government controlled by the Democrats." (TV, 5/9/94)

REALITY: Clinton is the fourth president since 1960 whose party has had a majority in both houses of Congress. Seven of the last eleven presidents have led party majorities in both houses for at least part of their terms. As for Democratic "control" of the third branch of government, the judiciary, eight of nine Supreme Court justices and about 70 percent of federal judges—including Limbaugh's uncle—were Republican appointees at the time Limbaugh made his claim.

LIMBAUGH: "I have to keep saying this. The Democrats have majority positions in both houses. . . . The Republicans can vote against anything and if there's Democratic unity it will sail through." (TV, 7/27/94)

REALITY: Since the GOP had more than 40 Senate seats in 1993–94, Republican unity behind a threat of filibuster (blocking a vote by holding the floor indefinitely) could prevent any Democratic proposal—even if there was "Democratic unity"—from "sailing through" the Senate.

JUST AN ENTERTAINER?

Unlike many of Limbaugh's claims, there's actually a grain of truth to it when he refers to himself as "the fourth branch of government." He has become a power to contend with in Washington. Conservatives on Capitol Hill see him as one of their most potent weapons; moderates and liberals are intimidated by him and his millions of devotees, many of whom stand ready to clog up phone and fax lines the moment they get the signal from Limbaugh.

The power of this one man to mobilize activists may outstrip that of the National Rifle Association or the American Association of Retired People (AARP). For while these groups have millions of members, what they lack is the broadcast power to reach their constituents each and every weekday. Even in liberal cities, broadcast stations have given that power overwhelmingly to Limbaugh and other conservative talkshow hosts (and rarely to advocates for consumers, the environment, feminism, seniors, etc.).

Perhaps it's because Limbaugh fears calling attention to this politically lopsided distribution of broadcast opinion power that he tries—usually halfheartedly—to downplay his ability to mobilize. On these occasions, he says: "I'm just an entertainer," or "I do not urge people to call Washington," or "I don't give out phone numbers." Hearing such denials on "Nightline," regular Limbaugh listener Ted Koppel objected: "You don't have to hand out a telephone number to suggest to your audience, look, if you have half a brain, you're going to let folks in Congress and folks in the White House know how you feel about these things." Absolutely right, Limbaugh acknowledged.

"You people in New Jersey. I want to tell you something. You have a huge responsibility on your hands because let me tell you what's at stake here. If you reelect Jim Florio, you are sending a message to every politician in this country that they can promise to cut your taxes, break the promise, and then raise your taxes all over the place, and you won't care. Now I don't take sides in political races, as you well know." (Laughter) *"That wouldn't be fair. It would compromise my objectivity as a journalist."* *(TV, 10/28/93, days before the election)*

One of the most revealing sources of information on his political clout is *Rush To Us: Americans Hail Rush Limbaugh*, a worshipful, insiders' book by two right-wing journalists about Limbaugh and the dittohead subculture. In the book, conservative activists, leaders, and members of Congress credit Limbaugh as the key player in stopping everything from Bill Clinton's job stimulus package to the Fairness Doctrine to a proposal that conservatives claimed would require federal certification of home-school teachers. Representative Bill Paxon (R-NY) comments: "We received a thousand calls" the day after Limbaugh addressed the obscure home-schooling issue.

On a daily basis, conservative lawmakers brief Limbaugh by phone or fax on issues around which they want him to mobilize pressure on Congress. "Senators and congressmen all across the board on the Republican side call him all morning long before he goes on," relates Republican strategist Mary Matalin. Newt Gingrich, who faxes Limbaugh regular briefings for the Republican leadership, says: "Every day he educates about six million people around the country who then become centers of communication." Says Limbaugh, "I don't call politicians; they call me." He's played a major role in getting Republican measures passed, even on previously arcane procedural issues like strengthening the congressional discharge petition (which can force bills out of committee).

In a major victory in October 1994, Limbaugh mobilized his listeners to help kill a bill that would have prevented members of Congress from accepting gifts and junkets from lobbyists. Forty-two senators changed their votes from yes to no. "It wouldn't have happened without Rush Limbaugh," commented a Gingrich spokesman (*Detroit Free Press,* 10/30/94).

Rush To Us summarizes the broadcaster's clout this way: "Limbaugh was the catalyst for a new politics that combined rapid-information technologies of the 1990s—fax machines and talk radio—with traditional grass-roots organizing to create a well-informed [*sic*], homespun but high-tech activism. He filled the airwaves with public policy talk traditionally relegated to a few slender columns at the back of newspapers. As a result, ordinary people . . . knew how to hit the right buttons in Washington—usually by starting with the ones on their phones." And, the book adds, "Limbaugh's show was a vital platform for affecting elections"—citing Limbaugh's on-air crusade on behalf of Republican Christine Todd Whitman, who narrowly defeated incumbent New Jersey Governor Jim Florio. According to Matalin, now a CNBC talkshow host, every Republican presidential hopeful for '96 calls Limbaugh to stay in touch.

Even conservative journalists—such as Terry Eastland in the *American Spectator*—suggest Limbaugh is not being honest when he claims, "I have no cause, no political agenda. I just want to be the best radio guy I can be." Such declarations are contradicted by the congressional staffer who was quoted on Limbaugh's TV show, marveling at "the amount of calls and mail he generates." And they're contradicted by his on-air endorsements of candidates and by the partisan statements he makes on broadcast after broadcast—like the time in May 1994 when he referred to the "crucial" upcoming election, expressing hope that "we can somehow reduce the Democratic majority in both houses."

On the day before the November '94 election, Limbaugh used his TV show to issue a call to action, urging his troops to "be ready at dawn tomorrow, dawn Tuesday" to work hard to "gain Republican control of Congress."

After the GOP election victory, Republican leader Vin Weber declared: "Rush Limbaugh is as responsible for what happened as any individual in America."

If he's just an entertainer, his "entertainment" may be the most narrowly partisan in the history of American broadcasting.

"To take a close look at Rush Hudson Limbaugh and his twenty million fans is to have one's hope in America's future restored."—Dan Quayle

6. Brotherhood . . .

LIMBAUGH: Defending himself against a charge of anti-Semitism: "I find it interesting that no one ever accuses Louis Farrakhan of being anti-Semitic." (Radio, 5/12/94)

REALITY: A Nexis computer search of news sources found some 3,000 articles mentioning Louis Farrakhan and anti-Semitism.

LIMBAUGH: "The videotape of the Rodney King beating played absolutely no role in the conviction of two of the four officers. It was pure emotion that was responsible for the guilty verdict." (Radio; *FRQ*, Summer/93)

REALITY: "Jury Foreman Says Video Was Crucial in Convictions," a *Los Angeles Times* headline declared after the federal court verdict (4/20/93). "It was the video, after a trial with 61 witnesses and more than 130 exhibits, that sealed the officers' fates, jurors said," the *New York Times* reported (4/24/93). "The tape put everything else together in a big parcel," a juror was quoted in the *Chicago Tribune* (4/20/93). "Without the tape there was nothing."

LIMBAUGH: On the Reginald Denny beating during the L.A. riots: "The media has never portrayed this as a race crime." (TV, 12/7/93)

REALITY: Many media reports portrayed the Denny beating as a racial crime. "Race was the motivation for the attack," wrote *Washington Post* columnist Richard Cohen. "Denny's beating, his near-murder, was a racist act. He was chosen for his race and beaten for his race." (10/26/93) *Chicago Tribune* columnist Clarence Page (10/20/93) called it "racist violence."

LIMBAUGH: "Clarence Thomas is a man who has escaped the bonds of poverty by methods other than those prescribed by these civil rights organizations. He has succeeded by relying on himself, rather than prostituting himself into the dependency cycle." (*Ought to Be,* p. 118)

*"I am incapable of telling you anything but the truth." (***Told You So,** *p. 158)*

REALITY: Thomas was admitted to Yale Law School under a 1971 affirmative action plan—the kind "prescribed by civil rights organizations"—whose goal was 10 percent minority students in the entering class, said Yale officials. Limbaugh's claim was contradicted by Thomas himself in November 1983 remarks to his EEOC staff in defense of affirmative action programs: "But for them, God only knows where I would be today. These laws and their proper application are all that stand between the first 17 years of my life and the second 17 years." (*Boston Globe,* 7/14/91)

LIMBAUGH: "So many people are either refusing to recognize or unable to recognize the difference between blacks who riot and the majority of blacks in the American middle class. According to University of Chicago sociologist William Julius Wilson, of the 29 million blacks in America, the largest percentage—35 percent—are upper middle class, both professional (lawyer, doctor) and white collar; 32 percent are middle class; and 33 percent are considered poor." (*Ought to Be,* p. 224)

REALITY: "Limbaugh's quote represents a great distortion," Wilson wrote in a printed statement about Limbaugh's claim. In a *Los Angeles Times* column (5/6/92), Wilson laid out his position on the class makeup of African Americans, saying that 20 percent of blacks are in the "professional middle class" (a category that includes teachers and nurses) and that a further 15 percent are in "nonprofessional white-collar positions" such as secretarial or sales jobs. Limbaugh deceptively combines these categories into one, and calls them all "upper middle class"—a description that hardly fits most teachers, let alone most salesclerks and secretaries. The category Limbaugh calls "middle class" Wilson had referred to as "working class," people who Wilson noted were "vulnerable to job loss through economic restructuring."

FORTY-ONE THOUSAND NOBODIES

A caller describes the new light rail system in St. Louis:

LIMBAUGH: I know St. Louis. Where does the light rail system go?

CALLER: It's running from downtown at Union Station out to the airport, and then there is one branch that runs to East St. Louis.

LIMBAUGH: (Laughing) East St. Louis? They got no light rail system to West County? They got a light rail system to East St. Louis where nobody goes . . . ? ! (Radio, 6/27/94; *FRQ*, Winter/94)

East St. Louis is home to 41,000 residents, 98 percent of them African Americans.

THE RUSH LIMBAUGH SHOW

LIMBAUGH: "Any time the illegitimacy rate in black America is raised, Reverend Jackson and other black 'leaders' immediately change the subject." (*Ought to Be,* p. 225)

REALITY: Along with many other black leaders, Jesse Jackson has been talking about and against teen pregnancy for decades. His 1987 compilation of sermons, speeches, and interviews *(Straight from the Heart)* contains numerous references to "premature pregnancy" and "babies making babies": "Our children are being programmed into premature heat, and the results are a teenage-pregnancy epidemic. . . . This 'intercourse without discourse' is jeopardizing the welfare of this and future generations." (p. 200)

LIMBAUGH: "Taxpaying citizens are not being given the access to these welfare and health services that they deserve and desire, but if you're an illegal immigrant and cross the border, you get everything you want." (TV, 7/5/94)

REALITY: Illegal immigrants have far less access than citizens do to health and welfare services. Although illegal immigrants pay taxes, they are ineligible for almost all federal and state programs, including cash welfare, food stamps, student loans, and federally funded health care, except for emergency treatment. (Congressional Research Service, 1993) An Immigration and Naturalization Service study released in 1992 found that less than one-half of 1 percent of illegal immigrants had fraudulently obtained food stamps or AFDC payments.

"I have a better recipe for Blacks' escape from misery than the civil rights leadership does: You make Black people listen to this show every day."
(Radio, **Flush Rush)**

LIMBAUGH: "There are more American Indians alive today than there were when Columbus arrived or at any other time in history. Does this sound like a record of genocide?" (*Told You So*, p. 68)

REALITY: According to Carl Shaw of the U.S. Bureau of Indian Affairs, estimates of the pre-1492 population of what later became the United States range from 5 million to 15 million. After centuries of European diseases, war, massacres, forced resettlement, and planned starvation, Native populations fell to 250,000 in the late nineteenth century. Today, fewer than 2 million people in the United States claim Indian ancestry, according to the Census Bureau.

LIMBAUGH: In praise of Senator Strom Thurmond (who'd called a gay soldier "not normal"): "He's not encumbered by being politically correct. . . . If you want to know what America used to be—and a lot of people wish it still were—then you listen to Strom Thurmond." (TV, 9/1/94)

REALITY: In the America that "used to be," Thurmond was one of the country's strongest voices for racism, running for president in 1948 on the slogan "Segregation Forever."

NO, I AM NOT A RACIST

"I am not a racist," protests Rush Limbaugh, who says he's affronted that the question keeps coming up. We offer a sampling of his own words.

To a black caller: "Take that bone out of your nose and call me back." (*Newsday*, 10/8/90)

"Have you ever noticed how all newspaper composite pictures of wanted criminals resemble Jesse Jackson?" (*Newsday*, 10/8/90)

On film director Spike Lee's request that black kids get off from school to see his movie *Malcolm X:* "Spike, if you're going to do that, let's complete the education experience. You should tell them that they should loot the theater, and then blow it up on their way out." (TV, 10/29/92)

"The NAACP should have riot rehearsal. They should get a liquor store and practice robberies." (Radio; *Flush Rush*)

Speculating on why a Mexican national won the New York marathon: "An immigration agent chased him for the last 10 miles." (*USA Weekend*, 1/26/92)

Discussing a Chicago inner-city schoolteacher punished for using a math question that focused on the price of prostitution and cocaine habits, Limbaugh suggested that the teacher should be credited for understanding "the culture these kids come from." The math question began: "Rufus is pimping three girls." (TV, 5/24/94)

Limbaugh refers to Somali leader as "the little guy that used to be the warlord, Mohammed Farah Aidid Saheeb Skyhook." (TV, 7/13/94)

On the discovery by Japanese scientists of a meat substitute derived partly from sewage solids, the "sewage burger": "I know where they could test this thing—Somalia!" (Radio commentary, 10/11/93)

He accompanies the mention of Senator Carol Moseley-Braun's name with the theme song "Movin' On Up" from "The Jeffersons."

To a caller who said that black people need to be heard: "They are 12 percent of the population. Who the hell cares?" (Radio, *Flush Rush*)

"They [Native Americans] were meaner to themselves than anybody was ever mean to them. These people were savages . . . Killing each other. Scalping each other." (Radio, 12/14/93)

Although Limbaugh was critical of Klansman-turned-Republican David Duke (because of his past and the "damage" he'd do to the Republican Party), a 900-number preference poll of Limbaugh's radio listeners the day before the 1991 Louisiana gubernatorial election (11/15/91) found that 82 percent said they would vote for David Duke. That's more than twice the percentage (39 percent) that voted for Duke in the next day's Louisiana election.

"To whatever extent this nation is racist, that racism is fueled primarily by the rantings and ravings and inconsistencies, the absolute idiocies of people like Jesse Jackson and Benjamin Chavis." (Radio, 6/4/93)

7. . . . and Sisterhood

LIMBAUGH: "Women were doing quite well in this country before feminism came along." (Radio; *FRQ,* Summer/93)

REALITY: Before feminism "came along" in the late nineteenth century, women couldn't even vote.

LIMBAUGH: To a caller who said she'd been fired for listening to Limbaugh's radio show: "I know the kind of woman who fired you. They are humorless. They are sourpusses. They are bitter and they go through life basically angry at the world."
CALLER: "Actually, she had a real good, fun personality."

(Radio, 1/12/94; **Flush Rush)**

LIMBAUGH: On Senator Bob Packwood: "What's the big deal? He's clumsy with women." (Radio; *Flush Rush*)

REALITY: Packwood has been charged by dozens of women with nonconsensual sexual advances, including reaching his hand up an employee's skirt, trying to remove clothing, sexual embraces and gropes, repeatedly forcing kisses on employees, and inserting his tongue in a staffer's mouth. Such encounters often ended only because of forceful struggle by the women. Packwood is also charged with intimidating and threatening to smear women who went public. (*Washington Post,* 11/22/92; *Chicago Sun-Times,* 11/30/94)

"We're in bad shape in this country when you can't look at a couple of huge knockers and notice it."
(TV, 2/2/94)

LIMBAUGH: "One of the 'expert' commentators for the networks during the televised [Clarence Thomas/Anita Hill] hearings was Catharine MacKinnon, a law professor at the University of Michigan. She was just a fringe feminist before the hearings, but being presented as an analyst by the networks accorded her 'expert' status." (*Ought to Be,* p. 126)

REALITY: MacKinnon wrote the definitive work on sex harassment in 1979: *Sexual Harassment of Working Women.* In 1986, she was co-counsel in the landmark *Vinson* case, winning a unanimous Supreme Court ruling that set the current legal standard for sexual harassment. During the 1980s, according to a *New York Times* profile (10/6/91), "MacKinnon may have had as much effect on American law as any professor in the country."

LIMBAUGH: "Anita Hill followed Clarence Thomas everywhere. Wherever he went, she wanted to be right by his side, she wanted to work with him, she wanted to continue to date him. . . . There were no other accusers who came forth after Anita Hill did and said, 'Yeah, Clarence Thomas, he harassed me, too.' There was none of that." (TV, 5/4/94)

REALITY: Hill could hardly have "continued to date" Thomas since, by both their accounts, they never dated. Two other women, Sukari Hardnett and Angela Wright, came forward immediately after Anita Hill to charge Thomas with similar behavior. (*Strange Justice* by Mayer and Abramson)

LIMBAUGH: Discussing David Brock, author of *Anita Hill: The Untold Story:* "They're doing everything they can to keep this book squelched. Authors go on TV to promote their books, right? You go on the 'Today' show. You go on whatever show to promote your book. With David Brock, they have refused to let him on TV unless somebody from the other side comes on to debate the issue with him; and the other side, being very smart, has refused to come on, thereby keeping Brock off the air. And the reason is because everything in [the book] is true." (TV, 5/10/93)

REALITY: Exactly one week before Limbaugh's broadcast, David Brock was on the "Today" show debating someone from "the other side"—Charles Ogletree, Anita Hill's lawyer. (Perhaps Limbaugh blocked all memory of the show, since Ogletree enumerated a litany of errors in Brock's book, as did the *New Yorker,* 5/24/93.)

LIMBAUGH: Quoting "Sheila Cronen, one of the feminist movement's most 'respected' leaders and spokeswomen": "The simple fact is, every woman must be willing to be recognized as a lesbian to be fully feminine." (*Ought to Be,* p. 189)

REALITY: Limbaugh gets the source of the quote wrong: It's not from Sheila Cronen, but from a column by Rosemary Dempsey and Sharon Fawley (*NOW Times,* 1/88). He garbles the quote: What the two women actually wrote was, "The simple fact is that every woman must be willing to be identified as a lesbian to be fully feminist." And he wrenches it out of context: The very next sentence explains, "We are not suggesting that every woman must live a lesbian lifestyle, but every woman must recognize that lesbian rights are fundamental to the women's movement."

"Sexual harassment at this work station will not be reported. However . . . it will be graded!!!"—sign on Limbaugh's office (USA Weekend, 1/26/92)

LIMBAUGH: "Now I got something for you that's true—1972, Tufts University, Boston. This is 24 years ago—or 22 years ago. Three-year study of 5,000 coeds, and they used a benchmark of a bra size of 34C. They found that the—now wait. It's true. The larger the bra size, the smaller the IQ." (TV, 5/13/94)

REALITY: Dr. Burton Hallowell, president of Tufts in the '60s and '70s, had "absolutely no recollection" of such a study, according to Tufts' communications office. "I surely would have remembered that!" he exclaimed. Limbaugh's staff was unable to produce any such study. A search of the Nexis data base, while revealing no evidence of a Tufts study, did produce a number of women theorizing that the presence of large breasts causes a lowering of IQ in some males.

PRO-LIFE OR PRO-LIE?

LIMBAUGH: "Feminists don't often put pro-abortion initiatives on state ballots, because they have lost more times than they have won." (*Ought to Be*, p. 58)

REALITY: Since the Supreme Court's *Webster* decision in 1989 gave the states power to restrict abortion, pro-choice groups have three times taken the expensive route of statewide ballot initiatives to protect abortion rights. The pro-choice side won each time: Nevada (1990), Washington (1991), and Maryland (1992). By contrast, "most anti-abortion ballot initiatives since *Webster* have failed," reported the *National Journal* (10/10/92).

LIMBAUGH: "Jane Fonda said recently that it is imperative to get the government out of women's wombs. Tsk-tsk. If she were honest she would admit that what she *really* wants is the government *in the womb*. . . . That's why she and her radical feminist sisters insist that the government counsel pregnant women on their abortion options." (*Ought to Be,* p. 52)

REALITY: Feminists did not "insist that the government counsel pregnant women on their abortion options"; they called for an end to a government *prohibition*—the Bush administration's "gag rule"—which prevented doctors who received federal funds from even discussing abortion options with their pregnant patients.

LIMBAUGH: On the 1993 shooting death of Dr. David Gunn in Pensacola, Florida, at the hands of an antiabortion activist: "No one in the pro-life movement condoned it and spoke in favor of it." (TV, 3/16/93)

REALITY: The day before Limbaugh's absolution aired, a national television audience heard antiabortion crusader Paul Hill condone the killing on the Phil Donahue show, declaring it "absolutely" moral. Dozens of leading "pro-life" activists signed Hill's petition defending "lethal force" to stop abortion—before Hill himself killed a doctor and his escort in July 1994.

LIMBAUGH: "When the French RU 486 pill was developed in the early 1980s, it wasn't just the pro-life people who initially opposed it. Many abortion activists also had qualms about it or even opposed it. Why? Because it took abortion out of the clinics where all the money was made and brought it into the privacy of a woman's bathroom. It was only when they realized that blocking the French pill would be contrary to their image that they switched sides." (*Ought to Be,* p. 56)

REALITY: Some abortion rights activists and feminists opposed RU 486 because of health concerns—and still do—but not because it would cut into clinics' income. RU 486 still requires a trip to a doctor's office or clinic, and according to Marie Stopes International, a London-based women's health provider, RU 486 abortions have generally cost 30 pounds *more* on average (about $44 more) than a conventional abortion.

I DON'T LOOK WOMEN WOMEN NO MOD NM

"*I am not a male chauvinist,*" says Rush Limbaugh, maintaining that he has contempt for feminist extremists, not women in general. But his on-air antics suggest differently.

One of his routines is to play Sandy Posey's 1966 ballad, "Born a Woman": "A woman's place in this old world/Is under some man's thumb/And if you're born a woman/You're born to be hurt . . ."—at which point, Limbaugh yells out: "She said hurt, not heard!"

Limbaugh brags that he was fired from a Top 40 station early in his career for violating the music rotation by playing the Rolling Stones' "Under My Thumb" every day. The lyrics celebrate "a girl who once had me down" but is now "a squirmy dog" who "does just what she's told."

Limbaugh announced on his national radio show that women who wanted to call in to the program should send photos of themselves. (*Newsday*, 10/8/90)

"I'm tired of hostile women. I'm tired of colleges that turn out female graduates that are prepared to be raped or beat up or discriminated against somehow, and are just waiting for some man to discriminate, take advantage, or be cruel, unkind, or whatever." (TV, 2/23/94)

"Feminism was established so that unattractive women could have easier access to the mainstream of society." (Limbaugh's "35 Undeniable Truths")

Describes a typical feminist as a "frumpy-looking woman who has been discriminated against because she is unattractive and hasn't found a decent guy to marry." (*The Rush Limbaugh Story*, p. 77)

"There are God-given roles. There is human nature. And what's happening here is that there's a group of people—for some reason, women—militant women—not all, that are upset with their God-given role in human nature, and they're trying to change it and trying to alter it, and you can't." (TV, 2/23/94)

After quoting Tipper Gore explaining that she gave up her career for the sake of her marriage, Limbaugh advises women: "If you want a successful marriage, let your husband do what he wants to do. . . . You women don't realize how fortunate you are to be watching this show. I have just spelled out for you the key ingredients to a successful marriage." (TV, 2/23/94)

Criticizing those who believe standardized entrance exams discriminate against girls as "angry at achievers": "They may not be studying as hard, working as hard [as boys]; they may not be as smart." (Radio, 2/17/94; *St. Petersburg Times*, 2/18/94)

"I think this reason why girls don't do well on multiple choice tests goes all the way back to the Bible, all the way back to Genesis, Adam and Eve. God said 'All right, Eve, multiple choice or multiple orgasms, what's it going to be?' We all know what was chosen." (TV, 2/23/94)

LIMBAUGH'S SPELL

Limbaugh's relationship to his followers has the feel of a cult. Although some of the cultlike rituals are performed in jest or parody, there remains a whiff of the totalitarian in the language of Limbaughspeak. Before parting with his fans for the weekend, Limbaugh offers a Friday homily: "Relax and forget everything and have a great time. I will devote my weekend to keeping track of all relevant events so that you won't have to . . ." He regularly tells his listeners not to read newspapers because "I will do all your reading, and I will tell you what to think about it." And his followers respond not with dialogue or challenge but with salutations of admiration: "dittos" and "megadittos."

There's an Orwellian flavor when his followers come together in one of over 100 "Rush Rooms" (in restaurants across the country, many "officially sanctioned" by Limbaugh headquarters) for lunch or brunch and booming broadcasts of Big Brother Rush. In a Florida Rush Room, a sign on the wall reads: "Thank you for being quiet during the broadcast of Rush's show. Feel free to talk during station breaks." (*St. Petersburg Times,* 2/18/94)

What is Limbaugh's magic? What's behind his unusual ability to attract and enthrall a huge audience with his political commentary?

In terms of content, Limbaugh is no pioneer. He treads an old familiar highway called "backlash," playing to resentments about racial minorities and upstarts who are said to go too far and demand too much (women, environmentalists, gays, etc.). If not for such groups, and the "liberal elitists" behind them, America would be great again, runs the refrain. Our country doesn't need reform so much as protection from the reformers. With such themes, George Wallace won 10 million votes for president in 1968, and Ronald Reagan swept the electorate.

But Limbaugh is a pioneer in his method of delivery. Unlike Wallace, he doesn't appear angry. Limbaugh, at first glance, seems to be enjoying himself (and wants his audience to enjoy it, too). Unlike Reagan, Limbaugh doesn't need a TelePrompTer or printed text to dazzle an audience. Limbaugh is chatty to the point of being a motor-mouth. Given that he's usually on the attack, his plunge-ahead delivery would get him into big trouble (as it did Morton Downey Jr.)—but Limbaugh has the uncanny ability to soar to the edge, and, most times, pull back. If he gets too shrill, he'll pull back with humor. If he gets too lewd for his "family values" show, he'll retreat with an apology. As long as you share at least some of his prejudices, the roller-coaster ride with Limbaugh can be great fun.

If Limbaugh does *not* confirm your prejudices (or if he does, but you possess factual details on issues he's speaking about), he's likely to come across as an obvious charlatan, thus illuminating the love/hate divide on Limbaugh that has disrupted families. To those not caught up in his spell, the Limbaugh roller-coaster ride—with cruel remarks followed by "Aw shucks, I'm just an entertainer" denials—produces few laughs and much nausea. His performance comes across in endless waves of hypocrisy and contradiction.

He denies being a male chauvinist and then refers to women professionals as "reporterettes" or "professorettes." He claims that criticism of right-wing Christian extremists is just "religious bigotry" but doesn't think twice about making fun of others' religious rituals, like the Hindu practice of chanting. He tells his audience day after day how conservatives are happy, well-adjusted folks, unlike liberals who are "bitter" and "whiny." And then he launches

"I picked up the phone and heard the unmistakable voice. Honest to God, my mouth went dry and my palms got sweaty. . . . No one, myself included, could believe it was actually him."

—Mary Matalin, Bush campaign official, describing her first call from Limbaugh (All's Fair by Matalin and Carville, p. 205)

into extended bitter rants, whining even about homeless people who return empty bottles to supermarkets: "They loiter around, wander through the aisles, and block checkout stands as they sort their junk. The markets are required by law to take in products for recycling, but they shouldn't have to put up with people who disrupt their businesses."

The deeper a skeptic looks into Limbaughism, the more he/she sees its incoherence and self-contradiction, such that almost every assertion seems to dispute something said immediately before or after. In his first book, for example, Limbaugh rails against liberals as "a bunch of aggrieved weirdos who don't fit in," and in the very next sentences tells us that these misfits actually fit in too well: "They control many of our institutions, our universities, our major media outlets. They all have cushy jobs, they

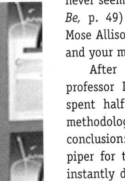

never seem to get fired or laid off." (*Ought to Be*, p. 49) Limbaugh's act often recalls the Mose Allison song: "Your mind is on vacation, and your mouth is workin' overtime."

After California Polytechnic University professor Donald Lazere (and his students) spent half a year investigating Limbaugh's methodology and accuracy, Lazere drew this conclusion: "Limbaugh is a frightening pied piper for the age of sound-bite politics and instantly disposable infotainment. Few of his listeners and readers seem to know or care when he is fabricating falsehoods, so long as he stokes their prejudices and assures them that they are smarter than those journalistic, scholarly, and scientific 'lamebrains' and 'nitwits' who bother to verify their data and put two ideas together in consistent order."

8. Dr. Limbaugh Will See You Now

LIMBAUGH: "There is no conclusive proof that nicotine's addictive. . . . And the same thing with cigarettes causing emphysema, lung cancer, heart disease." (Radio, 4/29/94)

RUSH LIMBAUGH, A 'TALENT' ON LOAN FROM GOD.

REALITY: Nicotine's addictiveness has been reported in medical literature since the turn of the century. Surgeon General C. Everett Koop's 618-page 1988 report on nicotine addiction left no doubts on the subject. When the *New York Times* (8/2/94) asked two independent experts to rank nicotine in terms of "dependence," both rated it ahead of heroin, cocaine, and alcohol. (Dependence was defined as "how difficult it is for the user to quit, the relapse rate, the percentage of people who eventually become dependent, the rating users give to their own need for the substance, and the degree to which the substance will be used in the face of evidence that it causes harm.") As for cigarettes causing diseases such as lung cancer and emphysema: "Today the scientific base linking smoking to a number of chronic diseases is overwhelming, with a total of 50,000 studies from dozens of countries," states *Encyclopaedia Britannica*'s 1987 "Medical and Health Annual."

LIMBAUGH: On the antismoking "tobacco gestapo": "It would have seemed to me that the time for hysteria would have been 1965, 1955—even 1975, before all these antismoking regulations hit. Now I think there used to be at the peak, something like 85 million or 90 million Americans who smoke—maybe more—maybe it's 100 million. But now it's down to 24 million. You would never know that, though, by judging the hysteria that's out there." (TV, 5/5/94)

REALITY: Limbaugh is blowing smoke. When smoking peaked in the mid-1960s, less than 60 million adult Americans smoked cigarettes. Today, after 30 years of antismoking education—er, hysteria—there are still 46 million adult U.S. smokers. Most new smokers are children aged 11 to 14, says the American Cancer Society.

LIMBAUGH: "The worst of all of this is the lie that condoms really protect against AIDS. The condom failure rate can be as high as 20 percent. Would you get on a plane—or put your children on a plane—if one of five passengers would be killed on the flight? Well, the statistic holds for condoms, folks." (*Ought to Be,* p. 135)

REALITY: A one-in-five AIDS risk for condom users? Not true, according to Dr. Joseph Kelaghan, who evaluates contraceptives for the National Institutes of Health. "There is substantive evidence that condoms prevent transmission if used consistently and properly," he said. He pointed to a nearly two-year study of couples in which one partner was HIV-positive. Among the 123 couples who used condoms regularly, there wasn't a single new infection. (*St. Petersburg Times,* 1/30/94)

If Rush Limbaugh were a father, one wonders if he'd give his kids the same advice about food that he regularly dispenses to his audience—ridiculing virtually every health concern about diet raised by scientists. He refers to the nutritionists at the Center for Science in the Public Interest as "a bunch of little, skinny, wiry little nerd types" (TV, 4/27/94). He pooh-poohs scientific concerns about high-fat foods, hot dogs, bacon, caffeine, etc.—while lampooning healthful trends toward more bran and fiber consumption, and a less meat-centered diet. When it comes to food, as with all other issues, take Limbaugh's pronouncements with a big grain of salt—though he probably believes barrels of salt are healthier for you.

LIMBAUGH: Commenting on a report released by the Center for Science in the Public Interest showing that popcorn cooked in coconut oil is high in saturated fat: "One press conference and a few sound bites and coconut oil is banned." Later in the same show, Limbaugh claimed that "coconut oil has been severely restricted." (Radio, 6/27/94)

REALITY: Neither claim is true. While managers of some movie theaters decided voluntarily to stop using coconut oil for their popcorn, no law or ordinance had "banned" or "restricted" coconut oil.

LIMBAUGH: "Apple growers use Alar to maintain a red robust color on apples, and it has been proven harmless." (*Ought to Be,* p. 258)

REALITY: Alar is far from having "been proven harmless." The EPA under George Bush proclaimed "zero tolerance" for the food additive—declaring any traces of Alar on food illegal—because of links between Alar residue and "life-threatening tumors." Groups that raised questions about Alar's safety included the National Academy of Sciences and the American Academy of Pediatrics.

LIMBAUGH: Denouncing Jeremy Rifkin of the Beyond Beef campaign as an "ecopest": "Rifkin is bent out of shape because he says the cattle consume enough grain to feed hundreds of millions of people. The reason the cattle are eating the grain is so they can be fattened and slaughtered, after which they will feed people, who need a high-protein diet." (*Ought to Be*, p. 110)

REALITY: Sixteen pounds of grain and soy are required to produce one pound of edible food from beef (USDA Economic Research Service). As for needing a "high-protein diet," the World Health Organization and U.S. Department of Agriculture recommend that from 4.5 percent to 6 percent of daily calories come from protein. Beef is certainly not needed to meet such protein recommendations: the amount of calories as protein in rice is 8 percent; in wheat it's 17 percent. (USDA *Handbook No. 456*)

LIMBAUGH: Incensed over a Burger King franchise that wanted to add vegetarian burgers to its menu: "Vegetarians are a bunch of weaklings who wouldn't be able to bench press 50 pounds after one of their meals. Ask anyone in the NFL." (Radio; *New York Review of Books*, 10/6/94)

REALITY: Many prominent bodybuilders and weight lifters are vegetarians—including the world-record holder in the bench press, Stan Price. "Mr. Universe" Bill Pearl won that title twice after becoming a vegetarian. "Mr. International" Andreas Cahling, a professional bodybuilder for 13 seasons, is a vegan vegetarian who eats no meat or dairy products. Vegan Spice Williams, an actress and bodybuilder, can not only "bench press 50 pounds" but she can also squat press Rush Limbaugh, as long as his weight stays below 315 pounds. ("Meatless Muscle," *Vegetarian Times*, 4/94) "Ask anyone in the NFL"? You might ask National Football League vegetarians, such as Philadelphia Eagles star receiver Calvin Williams, or 1991 Heisman Trophy–winner Desmond Howard, who plays for Washington.

POLITICAL ERRORIST

BALONEY

RUSH LIMBAUGH

HUCK/KONOPACKI LABOR CARTOONS

MISINFORMED ON HEALTH REFORM

LIMBAUGH: On health care: "We've been doing what we've been doing for 100 years and people have been getting along fine." (TV, 10/13/93)

Readers of Mad *magazine (10/93) voted Limbaugh the celebrity most deserving of "unnecessary root canal" treatment.*

REALITY: Little about U.S. health care resembles the situation a century ago. As late as 1929, all but a small percentage of medical expenses were paid directly by patients. Health insurance was rare until Blue Cross was formed in 1933. Most insured Americans today receive coverage through their jobs, a development that became widespread only during World War II. There are 63 million elderly and poor Americans enrolled in Medicaid and Medicare, programs that began in 1965. Today, most Americans are enrolled in HMOs or other forms of managed care, programs that were largely experimental until the HMO Act of 1973.

LIMBAUGH: "If you have any doubts about the status of American health care, just compare it with that in other industrialized nations." (*Told You So*, p. 153)

REALITY: OK, let's use the same standards Limbaugh uses to declare that "the health of the American people has never been better": life expectancy and infant mortality (*Told You So*, p. 153). Among 23 industrialized nations, the United States ranks 19th in life expectancy and 20th in infant mortality, according to the CIA's 1993 *World Fact Book*. Although it spends the most per capita on health care, the United States has the lowest health care satisfaction rate (11 percent) of the 10 largest industrialized nations. (*Health Affairs*, vol. 9, no. 2)

LIMBAUGH: "Most Canadian physicians who are themselves in need of surgery, for example, scurry across the border to get it done right: the American way. They have found, through experience, that state medical care is too expensive, too slow and inefficient, and, most important, it doesn't provide adequate care for most people." (*Told You So,* p. 153)

REALITY: "Mr. Limbaugh's claim simply isn't true," says Dr. Hugh Scully, chair of the Canadian Medical Association's Council on Healing and Finance. "The vast majority of Canadians, including physicians, receive their care here in Canada. Those few Canadians who receive health care in the United States most often do because they have winter homes in the States—like Arizona and Florida—and have emergent health problems there." Medical care in Canada is hardly "too expensive"; it's provided virtually free and covered by taxes. So many patients scurry across the border *to Canada* that provinces like Ontario are moving toward photo-I.D. health cards to prevent Americans from taking advantage of their free health care. (*Toronto Star,* 5/7/94; *Newsday,* 8/18/94)

LIMBAUGH: Extolling U.S. health care: "Ask anyone you know from a foreign country . . . which country is the envy of the world when it comes to health care." (*Told You So,* p. 153)

REALITY: According to a Gallup poll, only 2 percent of Canadians believed that the U.S. health care system is better than their own. (*Toronto Star,* 9/13/93)

LIMBAUGH: "So here's what I think Bob Dole ought to do. . . . Go to Clinton. Say, 'Mr. President, we'll negotiate with you. We'll give you a bipartisan health care bill as long as you get rid of this stupid universal coverage idea—because we're not going to support you on that. The American people don't want that.'" (TV, 9/5/94)

REALITY: The American people "don't want" universal coverage? A mid-July 1994 *New York Times*/CBS News poll found that 79 percent of respondents nationwide said it was "very important" that every American receive health insurance coverage (*New York Times*, 7/20/94). A July 14–17, 1994, ABC News poll showed 73 percent support for "universal health coverage." A July 23–26, 1994, *Wall Street Journal*/NBC News poll indicated that 65 percent of Americans said Clinton should veto any bill that did not include universal health care.

9. The Clinton Obsession

LIMBAUGH: Quoting the June 1994 CNN/*USA Today*/Gallup poll: "This is the first time in the president's presidency that his disapprovals are higher than his approvals." (TV, 6/8/94)

REALITY: The June 8 poll, which reported 47 percent disapproving, and 46 percent approving, of President Clinton's job performance, was the *eighth* time that the same Gallup poll reported that Clinton's disapproval rate exceeded his approval rate. Clinton's lowest previous rating occurred a year earlier on June 8, 1993, when 37 percent approved and 49 percent disapproved.

LIMBAUGH: On President Clinton's haircut at the L.A. airport: "Here's a man who based his entire campaign on class envy and class warfare. Then he gets into office and keeps Air Force One on the tarmac of Los Angeles International Airport for 56 minutes, backing up and delaying flights for his own convenience." (*Told You So*, p. 223)

REALITY: Clinton's famous haircut delayed only *one* plane—the press plane that always trails behind Air Force One. "According to Federal Aviation Administration records obtained through the Freedom of Information Act, the May 18 haircut caused no significant delays of regularly scheduled passenger flights—no circling planes, no traffic jams," *Newsday* reported (6/30/93).

LIMBAUGH: I am not calling the president names.
KEITH (a caller): You do it every day.
LIMBAUGH: Give me one example of calling him a name. . . .
KEITH: You've called him a liar, a fool, an idiot.
LIMBAUGH: Those are not names. Those are assessments of his character. They are not names. (Radio, 3/10/94)

LIMBAUGH: On the Clinton administration: "They're moving the country to the left. They're doing it in the most concentrated way that has ever been done." (TV, 5/9/93)

"Rush is extremely sophisticated, extremely smart . . . He's very serious intellectually."
*—Former Secretary of Education William Bennett (**Flush Rush,** p. 36)*

REALITY: At the time of this statement, Clinton had moved the country little in any direction, with few legislative victories. By comparison, in the first months of the New Deal, Franklin Roosevelt had propelled the country leftward with the Civilian Conservation Corps, providing jobs to thousands; the Federal Emergency Relief Act, awarding millions of dollars in relief; the Agricultural Adjustment Act, setting up farm subsidies; and the National Industrial Recovery Act, which established minimum wage and maximum hour guidelines and authorized billions for the Public Works Administration to invest in jobs. (Among many other more "concentrated" moves to the left were the American Revolution; the Civil War and "radical reconstruction" of the 1860s; the Progressive Era of the early 1900s; the civil rights/Great Society era of the 1960s.)

LIMBAUGH: On a slight increase in the number of people below the official poverty line in 1993 vs. 1992: "And this is after two years of the Clinton economic plan!" (TV, 10/9/94)

REALITY: In fact, it was after only a few months—at most. The first Clinton budget and economic plan was enacted in August and implemented in October 1993. The 1993 poverty statistic—which measured incomes from January (when Bush was still president) through December 1993—could hardly be blamed on the Clinton plan.

LIMBAUGH: On Hillary Rodham Clinton: "She has more power than anybody that's never been elected to anything in the country that I can imagine." (TV, 8/10/94)

REALITY: It doesn't take much imagination to recall such unelected powerhouses as J. Edgar Hoover and Henry Kissinger. And it would be hard for a First Lady to have more power than Edith Wilson, who became de facto White House chief of staff for months after her husband, Woodrow Wilson, was incapacitated in 1919. She controlled who would see the president, and what information and issues would reach him. One historian referred to her as "acting president."

LIMBAUGH: On a page of "Stupid Quotes" in the May 1994 *Limbaugh Letter* subtitled "Folks, I don't make this stuff up," the lead quote was attributed to Eleanor Clift on the "McLaughlin Group": "Hillary and Bill Clinton cheating on their taxes was a protest against the Reagan era tax breaks for the wealthy. . . . They knew . . . the IRS would catch up to them and tack penalties. . . . If more people had been as far-sighted and altruistic as the Clintons, we could retroactively erase the deficit." Limbaugh commented, "It's only May, folks, and we've got our Stupid Quote of the year."

REALITY: April Fool! The item came from the April 1, 1994 issue of the right-wing newsletter *Notable Quotables*. Each item in the newsletter was dated April 1 and the issue signed off with the words "April Fools." (The *Limbaugh Letter* later printed a correction on this and another April Fools quote used as fact.)

Senator John McCain (R-AZ): "The best thing that's happened in the United States of America is Rush Limbaugh." (TV, 8/16/93)

LIMBAUGH: "You know the Clintons send Chelsea to the Sidwell Friends private school. . . . A recent eighth-grade class assignment required students to write a paper on 'Why I Feel Guilty Being White.' . . . My source for this story is CBS News. I am not making it up." (Radio; *Chicago Sun-Times,* 1/16/94)

REALITY: Ellis Turner, the assistant head of Sidwell school, says he has repeatedly looked into the story and found no evidence of such an assignment. "It's apocryphal," he concludes. The essay topic would be particularly difficult for the roughly 25 percent of the school's students who are not white. Limbaugh's source was *not* CBS News—it was CBS Morning Resource, an infotainment tip sheet for talk-show hosts that has no more relationship to CBS's news division than a CBS game show does. The tip sheet, which compiles items from other sources, attributed the item to *Playboy;* Limbaugh apparently didn't think *Playboy* would sound as credible to his listeners as CBS News would. The original source for the story appears to be *City Paper* (7/16/93), a D.C. weekly, which cited an anonymous, disgruntled parent of a Sidwell student, who later changed his account of the alleged essay to "Should White People Feel Guilty?" (*Washington Times,* 10/11/94; *EXTRA!,* 9–10/94)

TO BALANCE THIS CARTOON'S PREVIOUS CRITICISMS, WE'RE LETTING *RUSH LIMBAUGH* SPEAK FOR *HIMSELF* THIS WEEK... FOR INSTANCE, ON THE SUBJECT OF HIS OWN *ENORMOUS INFLUENCE,* RUSH HAS *THIS* TO SAY:

"I'M THE FOURTH BRANCH OF GOVERNMENT. WHY AM I THE FOURTH BRANCH OF GOVERNMENT? BECAUSE THE *OTHER TWO* LET IT HAPPEN!"

ALL QUOTES 100% GENUINE!

RUSH RECENTLY VISITED NEW YORK'S MUSEUM OF MODERN ART FOR THE FIRST TIME (FOR A SOCIAL FUNCTION)--AND LATER HAD THIS THOUGHT ABOUT THE IMPORTANCE OF *ART* AND *CULTURE* TO A *WELL-ROUNDED LIFE:*

"I DON'T GO TO MUSEUMS BECAUSE THEY DON'T HAVE *GOLF CARTS...* IF YOU PUT A GOLF CART IN A MUSEUM I'LL GO-- YOU CAN DRIVE AROUND IT A LOT FASTER!"

DURING THE *NAFTA* BATTLE, RUSH WEIGHED IN WITH *THIS* WELL-REASONED ARGUMENT...

"IF WE ARE GOING TO START REWARDING NO SKILLS AND STUPID PEOPLE. I'M SERIOUS. LET, LET, LET THE UNSKILLED JOBS, LET THEM, LET, LET, LET, THE, THE, THE KINDS OF JOBS THAT, THAT, THAT TAKE ABSOLUTELY NO KNOWLEDGE WHATSOEVER TO DO. LET STUPID AND UNSKILLED MEXICANS DO THAT WORK..."

FINALLY, LET'S CLOSE WITH SOME FOOD FOR THOUGHT FROM THE MAN WHO REGULARLY RAILS AGAINST "FEMINAZIS," "ENVIRONMENTAL WACKOS," AND "UGLO-AMERICANS":

"WHEN LIBERALS LACK A SUBSTANTIVE ARGUMENT--"

"--THEY RESORT TO *NAME-CALLING!*"

A TIP OF THE PEN (GUIN) TO THE *FLUSH RUSH QUARTERLY,* POB 270525, SAN DIEGO, CA 92198

WHITEWATER UNDER THE BRIDGE

LIMBAUGH'S RUMOR-MONGERING

Ted Koppel's special on press coverage of Whitewater (ABC "Viewpoint," 4/19/94) was a perfect opportunity to take Rush Limbaugh to task for spreading unfounded conspiracy theories. Instead, ABC journalists Koppel and Jeff Greenfield let Limbaugh off the hook.

On his March 10 radio broadcast, Limbaugh had announced the following in urgent tones: "OK, folks, I think I got enough information here to tell you about the contents of this fax that I got. Brace yourselves. This fax contains information that I have just been told will appear in a newsletter to Morgan Stanley sales personnel this afternoon. . . . What it is is a bit of news which says . . . there's a Washington consulting firm that has scheduled the release of a report that will appear, it will be published, that claims that Vince Foster was murdered in an apartment owned by Hillary Clinton, and the body was then taken to Fort Marcy Park."

After he returned from a commercial break, Limbaugh began referring to the story as a "rumor," but continued to claim that the story was that "the Vince Foster suicide was not a suicide."

Limbaugh was referring to an item in a newsletter put out by the Washington, D.C., firm of Johnson Smick International. The newsletter, relating a rumor that had no apparent basis in fact, reported that the suicide of White House attorney Foster occurred in an apartment owned by White House associates, and that his body was moved to the park where it was found.

Limbaugh took this baseless rumor from a small insiders' newsletter and broadcast it to his radio audience of millions, adding his own new inaccuracies: The newsletter did not report—as Limbaugh claimed—that Foster was murdered, or that the apartment was owned by Hillary Rodham Clinton. Limbaugh's dissemination of an unfounded rumor has been credited with contributing to a plunge in the stock market on the day it was aired (*Chicago Tribune*, 3/11/94; *Newsweek*, 3/21/94).

Appearing as an "expert" on the "Viewpoint" special, Limbaugh denied touting the story: "Never have I suggested that this was murder," he said. ABC's Jeff Greenfield, in a taped segment, further covered for the talkshow host, claiming that Limbaugh "broadcast the rumor as an example of the more wild stories circulating."

Later in the broadcast, host Ted Koppel also stuck up for Limbaugh when his role in spreading the story was challenged. "As I recall," Koppel said, "you didn't present it as accurate, did you? You represented it as one of the rumors that was going around."

The executive producer of Limbaugh's TV show, Roger Ailes, didn't claim that his star had questioned the rumor—he boasted, on the Don Imus radio show, that Limbaugh's report of "a suicide cover-up, possibly murder" was a scoop.

But Limbaugh doesn't seem as proud of his scoop. When a caller to the radio show that same day (3/10/94), identifying himself as a pediatrician from Memphis, articulately criticized Limbaugh for spreading false reports about Vince Foster's death, the host seemed to take it personally: "One thing I'm not is a rumor-monger."

Limbaugh later went on to imply that the pediatrician—Keith from Memphis—had been calling from the "West Wing of the White House" (even though he had also criticized the Clinton health care plan and endorsed a Canadian-style health system). "I think that what is going to happen during the course of this year," Limbaugh said, "is that a bunch of people are going to call this show that have been given marching orders. . . . What's going to happen is there will be numerous attempts, and they've gone on all the time, to discredit what occurs on this program."

The next day, apparently still smarting from the Memphis caller's remarks, Limbaugh instructed his staff on the air: "You guys be on the lookout in there for more calls from the White House disguised as pediatricians from Memphis."

FAIR associate Jonathan Eagleman tracked down the "Memphis pediatrician" and found that he was . . . a Memphis pediatrician. The pediatrician had received a number of hate calls from outraged dittoheads—apparently some of them hadn't believed their leader's claim that he was actually calling from the White House.

TOXIC MAILBAG

For a broadcaster who engages in personal attacks, Rush Limbaugh is remarkably thin-skinned. When a conservative journalist raised minor criticisms of him, Limbaugh denounced the writer as "one more of these little gnats out there trying to sink a Boeing 747." Where others might see sporadic scrutiny of an influential national figure, Limbaugh sees conspiracy. His explosive reaction against critics (to Limbaugh, they're all in league with each other) is a bit reminiscent of a schoolyard bully who finally encounters some resistance.

Limbaugh's defenders display a similar double standard. The pro-Limbaugh book, *Rush To Us*, derides the critical *Flush Rush Quarterly* as a publication that "relied chiefly on negative personal attacks." The book ignores Limbaugh's remarks lampooning people like Amy Carter and Chelsea Clinton for their appearance, but it quotes Limbaugh supporter Sam Francis, a *Washington Times* editor, as dismissing the quarterly's anti-Limbaugh gibes as "transparent, invalid, and mean-spirited. . . . There were jokes about Limbaugh being fat."

Confused about the difference between Limbaugh's (good) insults and his opponents' (bad) ones? Sam Francis explains that he and Limbaugh are simply misunderstood: "When we make fun of poor people or handicapped people, we're not literally making fun of them. We're trying to break the icon the Left is trying to create around these types of people."

No one is more ferociously intolerant of criticism of Limbaugh than a certain hard core among his followers. Ask any journalist who has uttered a negative word about Limbaugh, and they'll tell

you of the avalanche of calls and letters they've received, some downright threatening. While many Limbaugh fans may be rational, some kernel of his audience makes up a cultlike following that reacts to criticism with rage and an eerie protectiveness (as if they sense Limbaugh's own insecurity). For listeners supposedly steeped in family values, the vulgarity of their language is something to behold.

After Michael Gartner used a small portion of a *USA Today* column to criticize Limbaugh (7/12/94), he received a torrent of toxic mail from dittoheads—which provided material for a later column: "Mail Full of Hate" (*USA Today*, 8/9/94). Two different letter writers expressed a desire to urinate on his grave. A couple of notes called him a "kike." (He's not Jewish.) One letter mentioned Gartner's teenage son Chris, who had died weeks earlier from a sudden attack of juvenile diabetes: "Please don't take too long to follow Chris." When columnist Anna Quindlen criticized Limbaugh, she received "boxes and boxes" of mail. According to Quindlen's assistant, Elizabeth Cohen, some of it was "real racist and anti-Semitic stuff from people who admit they belong to the Klan."

Journalists need not express an opinion against Limbaugh to outrage his fans. Merely stating a fact is enough. After CBS News executive Larry Cooper had a letter published in *USA Today* pointing out that Limbaugh was wrongly identifying CBS News as the source of one of his false claims (about Chelsea Clinton's school), his workday was disrupted by angry phone calls from dittoheads.

Sometimes the hate pursues even nonjournalists . . . into their homes. When Limbaugh falsely characterized a Louisville nurse as a "transsexual lesbian," the woman began receiving threatening phone calls (see page 108). For Susanne Freeman of San Francisco, it took venomous notes from two different anonymous letter writers before she figured out what had triggered them: She realized—after scurrying through back issues of her newspaper—that her letter to the editor criticizing Limbaugh's inaccuracies had actually been published.

It's not easy to summarize the hate calls and letters (and manure) received by Brian Keliher, editor of *Flush Rush Quarterly*, because they never stop: over ten death threats and continuous obscene calls, replete with images of rape and violence. Noting that Limbaugh refers to his followers as "happy, carefree, and compassionate," the *Quarterly* now devotes a page of its newsletter to excerpts from the noxious communiqués. One letter denounced Keliher for, among other things, being Irish, calling him a "fatheaded mick." The anonymous writer added: "Some of the Irish (Buchanan, Buckley) overcame their nasty genes."

A more standard letter began this way: "Brian, You must be one real faggot. They and the rest of the freaks of the world are the only ones who oppose Rush. I would love to see you beaten bloody. Myself, when my friends and I go to Scum Francisco to beat up queers, we prefer to use the traditional thick broom handle. This is what I'll use on you if I get the opportunity."

After FAIR issued its report on Limbaugh, we received dozens of hate letters and calls, some loaded with gay-bashing and Jew-baiting references, and threats of violence. When we receive a new rash of such calls, we immediately turn up the volume on the Limbaugh radio show to catch his current tirade against us. Most hate calls we receive are from Limbaugh followers.

Might a fanatical listener actually resort to violence? Columnist Lars-Erik Nelson noted (*Newsday*, 2/24/94) that Ronald Gene Barbour, arrested in early 1994 for threatening the life of the president, is a dittohead who staked out Clinton's jogging routes armed with a Colt .45 automatic revolver. "I like Rush, I sure do," the self-described manic-depressive told a reporter from his jail cell. "I love his polemics on Clinton. He's a disgrace to the country. He should be where I'm at. He's a criminal."

10. Fractured History

LIMBAUGH: "Columbus saved the Indians from themselves." (Radio, *Flush Rush*)

"I am a profound success because I relentlessly pursue the truth, and I do so with the epitome of accuracy."
(Playboy, *12/93*)

REALITY: Columbus had the most direct impact on the Taino Arawaks, Indians who lived on the island of Hispaniola, where he served as the first Spanish governor. Within a few years of Columbus's arrival, tens of thousands of Tainos were dead, through murder, mutilation, and suicide. Within a few decades, conquest and slavery had exterminated almost the whole native population on the island, which modern historians estimate at between 60,000 and 250,000 inhabitants in 1492. (See *A People's History of the United States,* Howard Zinn; *London Times,* 5/6/93)

LIMBAUGH: "On August 1, 1620, the Mayflower set sail. It carried a total of 102 passengers, including 40 Pilgrims led by William Bradford. On the journey, Bradford set up an agreement, a contract, that established just and equal laws for all members of their new community, irrespective of their religious beliefs." (*Told You So,* p. 70)

REALITY: The Mayflower carried not 40, but 78, Puritan Separatists (Pilgrims). Limbaugh neglected to count the 38 Pilgrim women and children on board. Their leader was *not* William Bradford, but John Carver. The Mayflower Compact, composed by Bradford, said nothing about religious tolerance. In fact, it declared that the colony was intended to serve "the Glory of God and advancement of the Christian faith." Though referring to "just and equal laws," the compact did not provide political or property rights for women or servants. It was signed by the 40 males that made it into Limbaugh's history.

LIMBAUGH: "Why were people better educated before the American Revolution with no public funding than in 1993, when we are spending in excess of $100,000 per classroom?" (*Told You So*, p. 76)

REALITY: Before the Revolution, the overwhelming majority of Americans were illiterate.

LIMBAUGH: "This brings us to the Founding Fathers—the geniuses who crafted the Declaration of Independence and the U.S. Constitution. . . . Don't believe the conventional wisdom of our day that claims these men were anything but orthodox, Bible-believing Christians." (*Told You So*, p. 73)

REALITY: Several Founding Fathers were deists, like Thomas Jefferson, who crafted the Declaration of Independence. Anything but an "orthodox, Bible-believing Christian," Jefferson referred to such core Christian beliefs as the divinity of Jesus, his miracles, and resurrection as "mysticisms, fancies, and falsehoods." He referred to the Christian doctrine of the Trinity as "the hocus-pocus phantasm of a God like another Cerberus, with one body and three heads." Jefferson actually produced his own version of the Bible, "abstracting what is really [Jesus'] from the rubbish in which it is buried, easily distinguishable by its lustre from the dross of his biographers, and as separable from that as the diamond from the dunghill." (*In God We Trust*, Norman Cousins)

WASHINGTON COULDN'T TELL A LIE; LIMBAUGH CAN'T TELL THE TRUTH

LIMBAUGH: Quotes President James Madison: "We have staked the future . . . upon the capacity of each and all of us to govern ourselves, to control ourselves, to sustain ourselves according to the Ten Commandments of God." (*Told You So*, p. 73)

REALITY: Madison never uttered the quote, although it frequently appears in religious right literature. "This quote has been passed by us dozens of times," said John Stagg, editor of Madison's papers at the University of Virginia. "We checked into some of those sources but failed to find any source documentation." Says Stagg: "The sentiment is inconsistent with Madison's other recorded opinions."

LIMBAUGH: "In the late 1930s, America was looking at 22 percent unemployment rate. There was no such concept as welfare. There was no minimum wage guarantee. There was no 'safety net,' except the one that family members provided." (*Flush Rush*)

REALITY: By the late 1930s, a federal safety net had already been woven through the New Deal: relief, jobs, minimum wage standards, Social Security. The concept of welfare—at the state and local level—began in the last century. In the 1890s, New York City created public works jobs for the unemployed. By the turn of the century, state and local governments joined with private charities to fund housing programs, job banks, soup kitchens.

LIMBAUGH: On liberal "beggar-based" constituencies: "The Democrats have not had an administration to steer mass quantities of money toward them for a dozen years. Remember, the feminist, environmental, so-called civil rights groups, and Naderites were all sustained during the 1970s with federal funds or contracts." (*Ought to Be*, p. 307)

REALITY: Leaving aside the fact that Republicans controlled the White House for seven of the 10 years in the 1970s, groups in the above categories were definitely *not* "all sustained during the 1970s with federal funds." Many leading public interest groups have never solicited or accepted federal funds, including Greenpeace, the National Women's Political Caucus, and "Naderite" organizations such as Public Citizen, the Litigation Group, and the Center for Auto Safety.

LIMBAUGH: "I, for one, remember the long gas lines of the 1970s. . . . Those gas lines were a direct result of the foreign oil powers playing tough with us because they didn't fear Jimmy Carter." (*Told You So,* p. 112)

REALITY: The first—and most serious—gas lines occurred in late 1973 and early 1974, during the administration of Richard Nixon.

LIMBAUGH: On Iran-Contra special prosecutor Lawrence Walsh: "This Walsh story basically is, we just spent seven years and $40 million looking for any criminal activity on the part of anybody in the Reagan administration, and guess what? We couldn't find any. These guys didn't do anything, but we wish they had so that we could nail them. So instead, we're just going to say, 'Gosh, these are rotten guys.' They have absolutely no evidence. There is not one indictment. There is not one charge." (TV, 1/19/94)

REALITY: Walsh won indictments against 14 people in connection with the Iran-Contra scandal, including leading Reagan administration officials like former Secretary of Defense Caspar Weinberger and former national security advisors Robert McFarlane and John Poindexter. Of the 14, 11 were convicted or pleaded guilty, many to felonies. (Two convictions were later overturned on technicalities—including that of occasional Limbaugh substitute host Oliver North.)

IF YOU REMEMBER THE 1960s, YOU'RE NOT RUSH LIMBAUGH

LIMBAUGH: "And it was only 4,000 votes that—had they gone another way in Chicago—Richard Nixon would have been elected in 1960." (TV, 4/28/94)

REALITY: Kennedy won the 1960 election with 303 electoral votes, vs. 219 for Nixon. Without the 27 electoral votes from Illinois, Kennedy would still have won, 276 to 246.

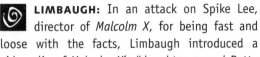

LIMBAUGH: In an attack on Spike Lee, director of *Malcolm X*, for being fast and loose with the facts, Limbaugh introduced a video clip of Malcolm X's "daughter named Betty Shabazz." (TV, 11/17/92)

REALITY: Betty Shabazz is Malcolm X's widow.

LIMBAUGH: "The liberals sit out there and suggest, as [Congressman] Vic Fazio did, that it is the radical right that's acting in a stealth manner. And the Christians and the religious right are about to take over America. Note that Mr. Fazio probably had no trouble with the Reverend Dr. Martin Luther King when he entered the political fray. The Democrats had no trouble with the Berrigan brothers during the Vietnam War era, and they were priests. The Democrats had no trouble with Jerry Rubin and Abbie Hoffman entering the political fray and running the Students for a Democratic Society. In short, Democrats have never had any problem with liberal religious people being involved in politics." (Radio, 7/11/94)

REALITY: Representative Vic Fazio probably *didn't* have any trouble with Martin Luther King's "entering the political fray"— Fazio was 12 at the time the Montgomery bus boycott brought King to national prominence. But Democratic leaders of the 1960s certainly had a problem with King: He was wiretapped by President John Kennedy and his brother, Attorney General Robert Kennedy. Federal harassment of King intensified under Democratic President Lyndon Johnson.

"The Democrats had no trouble with the Berrigan brothers"? In fact, the Berrigans gained national attention through highly publicized protests against Johnson's Vietnam policies. Jerry Rubin and Abbie Hoffman were hardly religious leaders; they led the political prankster/protesters known as Yippies, not SDS. And no serious observer of the 1960s could claim that "the Democrats had no trouble" with the Yippies, who were most famous for sparking demonstrations at the 1968 Democratic Convention in Chicago.

LIMBAUGH: On how to stop riots: "Richard Daley, in 1968, in the Democratic National Convention, issued an order—where there were rumors of riots—he issued a shoot-to-kill order. And there were no riots and there was no civil disobedience and no shots were fired and nobody was hurt. And that's what ought to happen." (TV, 6/10/93)

REALITY: Mayor Daley's shoot-to-kill order was issued not at the Democratic Convention but following the April 4, 1968 assassination of Martin Luther King. Daley wasn't reacting to "rumors of riots," since riots had already broken out. The shoot-to-kill order hardly put an end to unrest—four months after Daley's order, protestors flocked to Chicago's Democratic Convention and engaged in tumultuous civil disobedience.

LIMBAUGH: Referring to street disturbances at the 1968 Democratic Convention in Chicago: "Rolling Stones even recorded a song about it called 'Street Fighting Man.' . . . Maybe some of the renegades and rowdies that were trying to burn down Chicago are now in the [Clinton] administration at one level or another." (TV, 7/21/94)

REALITY: "Street Fighting Man" couldn't have been about Chicago, since the Rolling Stones released it in the United States a month *before* the convention. The federally appointed Walker Commission that investigated the Chicago disturbances reported no accounts of protesters "trying to burn down Chicago." Although there's no evidence of Chicago arsonists in the Clinton administration, some White House staffers are reportedly Rolling Stones fans.

Referring to the 1969 Woodstock festival: "Who said the '60s kids looked good and smelled good? Not all of them smelled good. If you were at Woodstock, you would know what I mean. And I wasn't there. But I saw pictures." (Radio, **Flush Rush***)*

RUSH TO WAR

LIMBAUGH: "We weren't driving the arms race, the Soviets were. They were the ones who continued to modernize and build up." (*Ought to Be,* p. 234)

REALITY: Since 1945, when the United States was the first to build (and use) the atomic bomb, America has consistently been first in developing and deploying new nuclear arms technologies—including the hydrogen bomb, intercontinental ballistic missiles, multiple-warhead missiles, submarine-launched missiles, and cruise missiles. (Center for Defense Information, Washington, D.C.)

LIMBAUGH: Explaining why the Democrats wanted to "sabotage" President Bush with the 1990 budget deal: "Now, here is my point. In 1990, George Bush was president and was enjoying a 90 percent plus approval rating on the strength of our victories in the Persian Gulf War and cold war." (*Ought to Be,* p. 304)

REALITY: Here is our point: In October 1990, when the budget deal was concluded, the Gulf War had not yet been fought. It wasn't until March 1991, after the war, that Bush enjoyed an approval rating of 90 percent.

LIMBAUGH: On the Gulf War: "Everybody in the world was aligned with the United States except who? The United States Congress." (TV, 4/18/94)

REALITY: Both houses of Congress voted to authorize the United States to use force against Iraq.

LIMBAUGH: On Al Gore's criticism of Oliver North's campaign remark that "Bill Clinton is not my commander in chief": "Al Gore actually lost his mind, went nuts. Everybody in the Democratic Party went loco-weed on this. And they started attacking Ollie's patriotism. 'How dare he criticize the U.S. government, the U.S. military.' . . . I found it just amazing because these are the same guys, Gore and Gephardt and everybody else, who threatened to withhold funding from troops in the Gulf War if the President [Bush] didn't get their permission for the use of force." (TV, 10/18/94)

REALITY: Who's loco-weed? Then Sen. Al Gore voted *against* a resolution that insisted President Bush needed Congressional authorization before waging war against Iraq. (1/12/91) Gore consistently voted in support of Bush on the Gulf crisis.

LIMBAUGH: On Bosnia: "For the first time in military history, U.S. military personnel are not under the command of United States generals." (TV, 4/18/94)

REALITY: That's news to the Pentagon. "How far back do you want to go?" asked Commander Joe Gradisher, a Pentagon spokesperson. "Americans served under Lafayette in the Revolutionary War." Gradisher pointed out several famous foreign commanders of U.S. troops, including France's Marshal Ferdinand Foch, in overall command of Allied troops during World War I. In World War II, Britain's General Montgomery led U.S. troops in Europe and North Africa, while another British general, Lord Mountbatten, commanded the China-Burma-India theater.

11. It's a Mad, Mad, Mad World

LIMBAUGH: On his 1993 conversation in Israel with Foreign Minister Shimon Peres: "He gave me some left-wing stuff—it's because of Reagan's tax cuts that we have fewer trees in the world." (*Limbaugh Letter,* 5/94)

REALITY: A spokesman for Peres wrote us that the foreign minister "has no idea whatever of the basis of such a statement, and that he has no inkling of what it is all about. He certainly does not recall making the statement ascribed to him."

LIMBAUGH: On Ben & Jerry's Rainforest Crunch ice cream: "There used to be a message on cartons of Rainforest Crunch ice cream that said that if you buy it, it will help Brazilian forest peoples start a nut-shelling cooperative that they'll own and operate. . . . The idea was to stop cutting down the rain forest in Brazil and instead get the Brazilian forest peoples, as it says on the label, to grow nut trees. . . . Not one Brazilian nut ended up in Rainforest Crunch. The nuts that are in Rainforest Crunch come, 90 percent of them anyway, came from established commercial suppliers." (TV, 9/29/94)

REALITY: Limbaugh's claim is nutty. Hundreds of tons of Brazil nuts have been used and continue to be used in Rainforest Crunch. But no one "grows" Brazil nut trees; Brazil nuts (not "Brazilian nuts") grow in the wild. While most of the Brazil nuts used in Rainforest Crunch have come from commercial suppliers—and some from a cooperative—they all have come from wild rain forest trees and were harvested by rain forest residents (mostly in Brazil, a few in Bolivia). As Ben & Jerry's has stressed, successful local nut ventures can forestall the cutting down of the rain forest.

LIMBAUGH: Addressing "U.S. businessmen trying to make money in Russia": "You're in the wrong hemisphere. You need to head to China." (Radio; *Flush Rush*)

REALITY: China and Russia are both in the Northern Hemisphere, and both in the Eastern Hemisphere.

LIMBAUGH: "When somebody wants to escape oppression, where do they go? The United States. The people fleeing Haiti did not go to St. Thomas or to Cuba. They tried to come to the United States." (*Ought to Be*, p. 214)

REALITY: St. Thomas is part of the United States—one of the Virgin Islands. As for fleeing elsewhere, more than 40,000 Haitians fled to the Bahamas, a country whose population is only 250,000.

LONG LIVE THE SOVIET UNION!

Describing the household Limbaugh grew up in, biographer Michael Arkush writes in the book Rush! *that Limbaugh's dad "with his loud, booming voice would rave for hours about the evils of communism." In the 1980s, Limbaugh himself raved for hours on the subject—to ever growing audiences. But well into the 1990s, Limbaugh couldn't seem to stop raving.*

LIMBAUGH: Referring to a power struggle in Russia: "You've got the old hard-line Communists trying to take control of the Soviet Union again." (TV, 9/22/93)

REALITY: The Soviet Union had ceased to exist in December 1991.

LIMBAUGH: "[Al Gore] thinks the automobile's more dangerous than nuclear weapons—and the Soviet Union is still aimed at us." (TV, 9/29/93)

REALITY: The Soviet Union—no longer aiming missiles at anyone—had ceased to exist in December 1991.

LIMBAUGH: On peace groups funded by Ben & Jerry's: "Probably a bunch of people out in California standing on top of Mount Shasta going 'Om, om,' trying to . . . send good vibes to Mikhail Gorbachev or whoever is running the Soviets so that they don't nuke us." (TV, 6/14/94)

REALITY: The Soviet Union ceased to exist in December 1991, at which time Gorbachev resigned.

12. New York, New York

Limbaugh has lived in New York since 1988 and pontificates as if he's an expert on the social and political life of the city. He's not.

LIMBAUGH: "The ex-mayor, General Dinkins—normally there's a six-month grace period—when you get defeated as mayor, you wait six months before you make a comment on the new mayor. Dinkins is now a lecturer at Columbia University. His first lecture was on how Giuliani's doing everything wrong. It's a first sign Giuliani's doing everything right, as far as I'm concerned." (TV, 2/21/94)

REALITY: Is there a grace period for disinformation? Ex-mayor Dinkins's professorship at Columbia didn't begin until September 13, 1994—nine months after Limbaugh's pronouncement. Dinkins did give a speech at Columbia in February, but it included only a brief mention of new mayor Rudolph Giuliani, a supportive comment: "To assist our new mayor is to help our city—we can do no less." (*The New Republic,* 8/8/94; *New York Times,* 9/14/94)

LIMBAUGH: Praising Mayor Giuliani while a *New York Post* headline is displayed: "'Drug Busts Up 14 Percent Since Rudy Took Over.' Drug-related arrests—and it's not because of a directive. It's not because there's been a proclamation from City Hall saying, 'I want drug busts up.' It's just that there's . . . renewed vigor in the police department." (TV, 2/21/94)

REALITY: In fact, it was a new directive that brought the change. Giuliani reversed a 20-year-long policy that avoided drug-related arrests by beat cops (aimed at reducing the temptations of corruption) and doubled the NYPD's permanent drug units. On his first day in office, Giuliani "strongly reiterated his intention to intensify the arresting of street-level drug criminals." (*New York Times,* 1/4/94)

LIMBAUGH: "Believe it or not, the cops in this city [New York] in previous administrations—when somebody, a citizen, complained about a loud radio or prostitutes on the corner or panhandlers or beggars harassing the neighborhood, the cops had to go to the Public Morals Squad, PMS. They have to go there to get permission to roust these people out of the neighborhood." (TV, 7/8/94)

REALITY: Don't believe it. According to the NYPD's Public Information Office, police officers have long had the authority to deal directly with such matters, and make arrests on the spot. They didn't need permission from the Public Morals Squad, whose narrow mandate is to investigate prostitution and gambling in support of cops on the beat. Detective Llanes told us: "Now and in earlier administrations, all you had to do is call the police, and they will move [prostitutes, panhandlers, etc.] along."

LIMBAUGH: "Frank Luntz of the Luntz Research Company did a survey of New Yorkers, asked them what's the most serious problem facing New York. [Reads list: crime/drugs, high taxes, unemployment, economy . . .] Show us number nine. 'Health.' Three percent of the people of New York are upset about health. So what's this crisis? Here [New York] is the liberal mecca. This is where Bill and Hillary get their message out unfiltered, unedited, and now in New York only 3 percent of the people who live here claim that health and health care is a bit of a crisis." (TV, 7/13/94)

REALITY: The survey by a Republican pollster didn't find that a mere 3 percent are "upset" about health care, but that 3 percent had identified it as the *single most serious problem*. Many New Yorkers consider health care a crisis: A New York *Newsday* poll (4/13/93) found that 44 percent of city residents thought health care was the biggest issue facing President Clinton, more important than the federal deficit or holding down taxes. As for the Clintons' ability to "get their message out unfiltered, unedited," Limbaugh ignores the fact that New York is home to two of the most effective Clinton-bashing dailies in the country, the *New York Post* and the *Wall Street Journal*.

LIMBAUGH: Referring to "commie" Daniel Ortega, then president of Nicaragua: "Peter, Paul, and Mary loved him and his wife. They had him up to their New York apartment (I never knew they lived together) back in the mid-'80s . . . and sang peace songs." (*Ought to Be,* p. 259)

REALITY: "Peter, Paul, and Mary never lived together," Peter Yarrow told us. The gathering in question was at Yarrow's home.

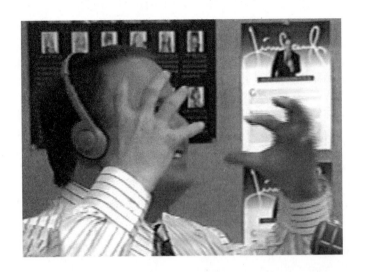

LIMBAUGH: "The president of the United States, Bill Clinton, came to New York on Wednesday, and he appeared at Cooper Union to make a big speech. Now you don't know this, but Cooper Union is just an arts and croissant school. It's not a big intellectual institution. It's not where presidents go—like the United Nations or something. It's just a traditional place here in New York. Abraham Lincoln made a speech there." (TV, 5/13/93)

REALITY: "Not where presidents go?" Clinton was the seventh president or future president (including Theodore Roosevelt and Woodrow Wilson) to speak at Cooper Union—a national forum since its founding in 1859. Clinton's speech would have been inappropriate for the United Nations, since it dealt with domestic economic policy. Far more famous for engineering and architecture than croissants, Cooper Union has long been a leading "intellectual institution." Past students include Thomas Edison, Felix Frankfurter, and Nobel Prize–winning physicist Russell Hulse. Past lecturers include Mark Twain, Victoria Woodhull, Jane Addams, Booker T. Washington, Andrew Carnegie, and William Jennings Bryan. Abraham Lincoln didn't just make "a" speech there; he delivered his 1860 "Right Makes Might" speech, which catapulted him to the presidency.

13. Stop the Presses

LIMBAUGH: On Whitewater: "I don't think the *New York Times* has run a story on this yet. I mean, we haven't done a thorough search, but I—there has not been a big one, front-page story, about this one that we can recall. So this has yet to create or get up to its full speed—if it weren't for us and the *Wall Street Journal* and the *American Spectator,* this would be one of the biggest and most well-kept secrets going on in American politics today." (TV, 2/17/94)

REALITY: We'll let Limbaugh in on the secret: The *New York Times broke* the Whitewater story on March 8, 1992, in a front-page, 1700-word report by Jeff Gerth. The *Times* published more than a half-dozen additional front-page Whitewater stories in the two months immediately prior to Limbaugh's utterance.

LIMBAUGH: On journalists' questions during the '92 presidential debates: "During the debates they didn't dare ask about foreign policy. That might have made President Bush look good. Can't have that. So they didn't ask about foreign policy." (TV, 5/12/94)

REALITY: Journalists *did* ask about foreign policy during the debates. For example, TV reporter Sander Vanocur asked about cutting U.S. military forces in Europe, and about U.S. interests in the post cold war. John Mashek of the *Boston Globe* inquired about China. ABC's Ann Compton asked about Bosnia and Somalia. Noting his avoidance of the Vietnam draft, UPI's Helen Thomas asked Clinton: "If elected, could you in good conscience send someone to war?" There were also questions focusing on foreign trade and foreign lobbyists.

LIMBAUGH: "The *Los Angeles Times* came out with a new stylebook and they had a lot of words that they said are now politically incorrect and we can't publish those words? And they were average, run-of-the-mill words. . . . Let's get a look at some of these words. . . . You can't say 'crazy' in the *Los Angeles Times* anymore. . . . You can't say 'zoo.' . . . I mean, we're not making this up. This is in the *Los Angeles Times*. You can't put 'divorce' in the *Los Angeles Times*." (TV, 5/12/94)

REALITY: In November 1993, the *Los Angeles Times* drew up a list of guidelines for words that may be considered offensive in *some* contexts. "Guidelines are meant to be just that: No words are banned," *Los Angeles Times* editor Shelby Coffey wrote in a memo to reporters (*Washington Post*, 12/18/93). That these words have not been banned is easy to prove: In the five months after the guidelines were issued and before Limbaugh made his statement, the word "zoo" was used 200 times and the word "crazy" appeared 935 times. The word "divorce" was not on the list; Limbaugh confused it with the word "divorcee." (Limbaugh was apparently not offended when Joseph Farah, as editor of the right-wing *Sacramento Union,* issued a rule in 1990 against such words as "gay," "assault rifle," and "women's health center"; Farah went on to ghostwrite Limbaugh's *See, I Told You So.*)

LIMBAUGH: "Marta Fitzgerald is my wife; met her on CompuServe. And by the way, it was not—listen, the *New York Times,* which never gets anything wrong, quoted my chief of staff, H. R. Kit Carson, who never spoke to them, and they quoted him as saying that we met on a computer dating service. This is why I don't want the press knowing anything about it. They purposely go out of their way to try to get things wrong where I'm concerned. It was on CompuServe, and I just simply got a letter from her one day that intrigued me, and it all started there." (TV, 6/6/94)

REALITY: "The couple met through the computer bulletin board CompuServe," the *New York Times* reported on May 30, 1994, announcing the wedding of Rush Limbaugh and Marta Fitzgerald. The *Times* never reported that the two met on a "computer dating service."

LIMBAUGH: Comparing the amount of news coverage of FAIR's report on Limbaugh's errors to that given the right-wing Media Research Center: "The Media Research Center has been around for years, and every two weeks they send out a newsletter called *Notable Quotables* in which they document factual errors and bias of the mainstream press. . . . Never, ever, is this stuff reported. The mainstream press never reports what the Media Research Center is saying. But they will, without checking, report whatever leftist media attack dog groups are saying." (Radio, 7/19/94)

REALITY: A Nexis computer search conducted at the time of Limbaugh's remark found more mentions of the Media Research Center (including 22 references to *Notable Quotables*) than of the "leftist media attack dog" in question, FAIR. *Notable Quotables* does not "document factual errors," but merely records quotes from journalists that the MRC views as biased. (The MRC has been "around for years," but not as long as FAIR.)

L I M B A U G H   V E R S U S   L I M B A U G H

Criticizing CNN reporter Bernard Shaw for saying, during the Gulf War, that journalists "can't take sides": "Can't take sides—! These were American journalists, and they can't take sides? That attitude illustrates the haughty arrogance of people in the news business." (*Ought to Be,* p. 272)

Two pages later: "The job of a journalist is to chronicle events, not stand up and cheer for one side or the other." (*Ought to Be,* p. 274)

CENSOR OR VICTIM
OF CENSORSHIP?

Few Americans can be said to enjoy freedom of speech more than Rush Limbaugh, with his 17$\frac{1}{2}$ hours of national broadcast time each week. Yet he constantly complains that he is a victim of persecution and "censorship"—at the hands of the Pentagon, Congress, gays, etc. On his TV show, the muzzled one even gave an award for "the best attempted censorship of me during 1993" to the Pentagon—*after* he'd become the most forceful partisan voice on Armed Forces Radio.

Limbaugh can be a stirring defender of free speech—when it's his own or that of someone he agrees with. Limbaugh calls his daily savaging of President Clinton the essence of patriotism, but that's hardly his position on criticism of former presidents Reagan or Nixon.

When a Limbaugh fan in Orange County, California, was dismissed from a Catholic high school after, among other things, accusing women teachers of "feminazi tactics" (in a school, ironically, where teachers would be fired for advocating abortion rights), Limbaugh used his broadcasts to defend the student as a martyred fighter for the First Amendment. That's also how Limbaugh hailed another high school student in Northern California who faced obstacles in setting up a Rush Limbaugh Club on campus: "My friends, we have here another classic example of discrimination and hypocrisy. . . . He's fighting for his First Amendment rights."

Classic hypocrisy, indeed. Calling himself Rush "Warmonger" Limbaugh, he had used his national radio show to applaud schools in Pasadena, Texas, that prohibited students from wearing peace symbols because school officials believed they were the mark of devil worshipers (*Washington Post,* 6/27/89). That same week, he denounced the Supreme Court ruling that flag burning is free expression protected by the First Amendment. And, during a public lecture, when his condemnations of artists Robert Mapplethorpe and Andres Serrano provoked a heckler's cry of "censorship," Limbaugh defended censorship: "It has been used throughout this nation's history as a means of maintaining standards." (*New York Times,* 12/16/90)

THE "HUSH RUSH" HOAX

"I, Rush Limbaugh, the poster boy of free speech, am being gang muzzled."

The broadcaster was crying censorship over congressional efforts in 1993 to reinstate the Fairness Doctrine, which he labeled "The Hush Rush Bill," "The Get Limbaugh Act" and "The Rush Elimination Act of 1993." Limbaugh's daily on-air crusade generated thousands of calls to Washington and helped derail congressional action. As usual, Limbaugh's followers were mobilized through misinformation and deception.

The Fairness Doctrine—in operation from 1949 until it was abolished in 1987 by Ronald Reagan's deregulation-oriented Federal Communications Commission—called on broadcasters, as a condition of their licenses from the FCC, to cover some controversial issues in their community, and to do so by offering some balancing views.

Reinstating the Fairness Doctrine can hardly be a "Hush Rush" bill aimed at silencing him, since it was broadly and actively supported on Capitol Hill *well before anyone in Washington had ever heard of Limbaugh.* In 1987 (when Limbaugh was still in Sacramento), a bill to inscribe the Fairness Doctrine in federal law passed the House by 3 to 1, and the Senate by nearly 2 to

RALPH NADER ON RUSH LIMBAUGH

(addressing the 1992 conference of the National Association of Radio Talk Show Hosts):

"Any talkshow host that has a pronounced agenda that's consistent, thematic, and focused—for example, Rush Limbaugh is clearly pushing George Bush—anyone who has a pronounced agenda like that seems to me has an obligation to expose that view to callers or to guests on the show. You can't simply say, as Rush says, he's only an entertainer. That's a cop-out. . . . But where you start naming names, attacking people,

1. Such "commie-libs" as Representative Newt Gingrich (R-GA) and Senator Jesse Helms (R-NC) voted for the bill, but it was vetoed by President Reagan.

In 1989 (when Limbaugh was just emerging as a national host), the Fairness Doctrine easily passed the House again, but didn't proceed further, as President Bush threatened to veto it. In 1991, hearings were again held on the doctrine, but interest waned due to Bush's ongoing veto threat. Yet when the same Fairness Doctrine emerged in 1993, with a new president who might sign it, Limbaugh egotistically portrayed it as nothing but a "Hush Rush Law." And his followers believed him.

And they believed him when he claimed the Fairness Doctrine was aimed at censoring conservative talkshow hosts: "It's the latest attempt by the United States Congress to legislate against me, and talk radio hosts." Remarked Limbaugh: "Why is 'fairness' so needed now? Because there's too much conservatism out there." In reality, not one doctrine decision issued by the FCC had ever concerned itself with talkshows. Indeed, the talkshow format was born, and flourished, while the doctrine was in operation. Right-wing hosts often dominated the talkshows, but none was ever muzzled.

The Fairness Doctrine did not require that each program be internally balanced or mandate "equal time." Nor did it require that balance in the overall program lineup be close to 50/50. It merely prohibited a station from blasting away day after day from one perspective, without opposing views. It would not "hush Rush," but it might get stations that offer only a constant diet of Limbaugh and fellow right-wingers to diversify their lineup a bit. Limbaugh was uttering nonsense when he said that to balance his show under the Fairness Doctrine, station owners "will have to go out and get two liberal shows. Or maybe three. Even three might not be enough." (Perhaps what Limbaugh meant to say was how difficult it is to find a host far enough to the left to balance his far-right views—especially since Mao is dead.)

A wide variety of citizen groups have used the Fairness Doctrine as a tool to expand speech and debate—not to restrict it. For example, it prevented stations from allowing only one side to be heard on ballot measures. (The abolition of the doctrine, a study found, had a disastrous impact on democratic debate around 1992 ballot measures.) Over the years, the doctrine has been supported by hundreds of grass-roots groups across the political spectrum, including the ACLU, National Rifle Association, and the right-wing Accuracy In Media.

"The Fairness Doctrine isn't going to take Rush Limbaugh off the air," remarked Larry King. "Be fair: What's wrong with that? If I were Rush, I would want a liberal host following my show."

Limbaugh argues that there should be no government "fairness" standards on broadcasters, since there are none on the print press: "You can buy a newspaper, and start it all you want, and they wouldn't dare try to do this [establish a Fairness Doctrine]" (TV, 9/17/93). He misses the key difference: If we want to compete with Limbaugh's publication in the marketplace of ideas, we can start our own publication right next to his. But if we set up our own competing broadcast program right next to a Limbaugh station on the radio dial—without acquiring a government license—we will be prosecuted. Broadcast frequencies are limited, and government licensed; printing presses are not. That's the legal underpinning of the Fairness Doctrine.

or representing a partisan political agenda in a systemic manner, I think there's an obligation to let some people in to challenge you and to have the two-way communication that is often associated with talk radio most prominently. He ought to be man enough to stand up to challengers and let them on [Enthusiastic applause from the assembled talk-show hosts]." **(The Rush Limbaugh Story, p. 202)**

RUSH LIMBAUGH ON RALPH NADER:

He's "a human handkerchief."

15. Lies About Myself

LIMBAUGH: Limbaugh frequently denies that he uses his show for political activism: "I have yet to encourage you people or urge you to call anybody. I don't do it. They think I'm the one doing it. That's fine. You don't need to be told when to call. They think you are a bunch of lemmings out there." (Radio, 6/28/93)

REALITY: One hour later, he was urging his followers into action: "The people in the states where these Democratic senators are up for reelection in '94 have to let their feelings be known. . . . These senators, you let them know. I think Wisconsin's one state. Let's say Herb Kohl is up in '94. You people in Wisconsin who don't like this bill, who don't like the tax increases, you let Herb Kohl know somehow." Week after week, Limbaugh encourages activism; he targeted congressmembers who hadn't signed a Limbaugh-endorsed deficit-cutting plan (6/30/94); encouraged calls to the Democratic National Committee about Hillary Clinton (7/16/94); repeatedly exhorted listeners to confront pro-Clinton health care caravans en route to Washington (late July 1994).

LIMBAUGH: On the suicide of White House aide Vince Foster: "Never have I suggested that this was murder." (ABC "Viewpoint," 4/19/94)

"The only difference between Watergate and Whitewater is that Whitewater has a dead body." (Radio, 3/94)

LIMBAUGH: Responding to President Clinton's complaint about Limbaugh's unchallenged broadcasting power: "I'm not on primetime anywhere, radio or TV." (TV, 6/27/94)

LIMBAUGH: Offering assurances to his radio audience: "I didn't talk about anything sexual with *Playboy*." (Radio, *Flush Rush*)

REALITY: From January through March of 1994, Limbaugh repeatedly suggested that Vince Foster's suicide was a homicide. For example: "The Vince Foster death—and I say death, not suicide. I'm choosing my word very carefully there. I really think there's something really rotten here." (TV, 1/12/94) On radio (1/27/94), he expounded at length on his doubts about the suicide note, the fingerprint and forensics evidence, the alleged lack of blood at the "crime scene." On February 3, he devoted most of a TV show to evidence that Foster was a homicide victim. On March 10, Limbaugh urgently announced a report "that claims that Vince Foster was murdered in an apartment owned by Hillary Clinton, and the body was then taken to Fort Marcy Park."

REALITY: At the time of this utterance, Limbaugh's TV show aired in primetime in several markets, including Dallas, Texas (9:30 P.M.); Albany, Georgia (10:30 P.M.); Brunswick, Georgia (10:30 P.M.); and Kingston, New York (9 P.M., rerun 11 P.M.).

REALITY: "Nice guys never get laid," Limbaugh complained to the *Playboy* interviewer.

CRITICS TO THE FRONT OF THE LINE?

Jim in Boston, a caller to Limbaugh's radio show (7/26/94), didn't offer the usual "megadittos." Instead, he told Limbaugh that he objected to the talkshow host's focus on the shortcomings of liberalism—never the shortcomings of conservatism.

But Limbaugh wouldn't enter into a discussion. "You, sir, are again using deception to get on this program," Limbaugh said, referring to the computerized message he had gotten from his call screener. "It says here that you wanted to talk about O. J. Simpson, DNA, and shaping the jury. Now, I'll tell you why this is important, is that no one has to lie to get on this program. If you would have said to the call screener what you just wanted to say, you wouldn't have been waiting here for as long as you had; you would have been moved to the top of the line."

"I did call your call screener," the caller replied, "and I did tell him the reasons, or the points I wanted to make, and he wouldn't accept the call. Now, since you do claim that you do talk to people who are going to be critical, I found no other way to get onto your show except by being deceptive."

Limbaugh's call screener denied that he had earlier rejected the caller, and Limbaugh hung up on him on the grounds that he had misrepresented himself.

Are callers critical of Limbaugh "moved to the top of the line," as Limbaugh maintains? You can test that claim by calling the show during airtime at 1-800-282-2882.

16. Limbaugh vs. Limbaugh

LIMBAUGH: "Rugged individualism does not call attention to itself. It simply achieves." (*Limbaugh Letter,* 3/93)

VERSUS LIMBAUGH: That same issue of the *Limbaugh Letter* is subtitled, "Dedicated to preserving my wisdom for the ages"; one section is described as "a sampling of my genius, to be widely quoted and disseminated." A full page is devoted to detailing his ratings and book sales, in order to demonstrate that "this [is] my era of dominant influence. . . . Naturally, none of this surprises me."

LIMBAUGH: First paragraph of book: "I was determined nevertheless to actually write the book, rather than farm it out to a ghostwriter." (*Ought to Be,* p. ix)

VERSUS LIMBAUGH: Second paragraph of book: "I chose as a collaborator John Fund, an editorial writer for the *Wall Street Journal* and a friend who shares my ideas and beliefs. This was crucial, for John's primary role was to interview me on tape, then write the first draft from the transcription of the interview." (*Ought to Be,* p. ix) In other words, exactly what a ghostwriter does.

LIMBAUGH: In frequent broadcasts, he offers impassioned advocacy for Paula Jones, who charged Bill Clinton with sexual harassment. (TV and Radio, April–May/94)

VERSUS LIMBAUGH: He boasted of a sign on his office door: "Sexual harassment at this work station will not be reported. However . . . it will be graded!!!" (*USA Weekend,* 1/26/92)

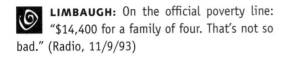 **LIMBAUGH:** On the official poverty line: "$14,400 for a family of four. That's not so bad." (Radio, 11/9/93)

VERSUS LIMBAUGH: A few months earlier, Limbaugh was talking about how tough it was to live on over 10 times that: "I know families that make $180,000 a year and they don't consider themselves rich. Why, it costs them $20,000 a year to send their kids to school." (Radio, 8/3/93)

LIMBAUGH: "All of these rich guys—like the Kennedy family and Perot—pretending to live just like we do and pretending to understand our trials and tribulations and pretending to represent us, and they get away with this." (TV, 11/18/93)

VERSUS LIMBAUGH: Limbaugh's 1993 income was an estimated $15 million. (*Forbes*, 4/11/94)

LIMBAUGH'S "FAMILY VALUES"

At the beginning of his first book, *The Way Things Ought to Be,* Rush Limbaugh hails "wholesome family values" as the key to a decent society. But Limbaugh's recurrent "family values" rhetoric is frequently contradicted by his actions. While criticizing premarital sex and ridiculing liberals for saying cohabitation is the same as marriage, he's lived with girlfriends before marriage. He denounces others over profanity and pornography, and then uses expletives in interviews with *Playboy* and *Penthouse* (and lies when questioned about it by fans).

He gleefully does a radio commercial for Hooters—a restaurant chain that promotes itself by emphasizing its waitresses' breasts—in an ad making light of the "shameless exploitation of women." He warms up his in-studio TV audience with a joke about prostitution. He extols the Ten Commandments, and then defends breaking the commandment against bearing false witness, as long as the untruths are told to the U.S. Congress.

While paying lip service to "family values," his comments about women are often crude, lewd, and lascivious. It's estimated that some 25 percent of Limbaugh's audience are Christian conservatives—which raises questions: For Limbaugh, is the rhetoric about "family" and "tradition" merely a means to attract that audience? And for his conservative religious followers, is Limbaugh's prurient talk excused as long as he affirms their political and social prejudices?

Here are some comments from the man who calls himself "The Epitome of Morality and Virtue," and pledges that he will not "tolerate smutty remarks on the air." (*Ought to Be,* p. 301)

Imputing some sort of sexual deviance to Anita Hill, he snickers: "My guess is she's had plenty of spankings, if you catch my meaning." (Radio; *The Rush Limbaugh Story,* p. 157)

"As you know, our Sexual Harassment Update theme on radio is 'My Eyes Adored You,' and we've changed the words to 'My Hands Explored You' *[audience laughter].*" (TV, 5/12/94)

On the air, Limbaugh asked a female camera operator, "Sandy, would you come and take the coins out of my pocket with your hand?" When she refused, he said this demonstrated that sexual harassment charges were overblown. After a commercial break, he persisted: "Sandy, if I would have stood up, would you have gotten the change out of my pocket?" (*Spy,* 5/93)

"We're in bad shape in this country when you can't look at a couple of huge knockers and notice it." (TV, 2/2/94; comment repeated with relish on TV, 2/7/94)

"I love the women's movement—especially when I am walking behind it." (*Ought to Be,* p. 146)

"If Madonna owned the Chicago Bulls or any other NBA team, you know, it'd give the whole term 'covering the spread' a whole new meaning." (TV, 3/22/94)

Female caller: "I do not mentally undress men."
Limbaugh: "Oh, come on! Everyone does." (Radio, *Flush Rush*)

LIMBAUGH: "There is a percentage of liberals, and especially the Hollywood left, who do not care anything for morality. They are not concerned about lies. Truth—the way most people understand it—is not a priority." (*Limbaugh Letter*, 3/93)

VERSUS LIMBAUGH: On the Reagan administration's deception of Congress: "It's okay to lie to Congress because they lie to us!" (Radio, 8/19/93) On Ollie North: "Let me tell you something. They say he lied to Congress. I can think of no better bunch of people to lie to than Congress." (TV, 6/6/94)

TO OGLE OR NOT TO OGLE: THAT IS THE QUESTION

Limbaugh's first book has a chapter on sexual harassment titled "To Ogle or Not to Ogle." In that chapter, Mr. Family Values smiles on men working at a radio station who allegedly made a game of pulling off women's underpants, and vigorously defends a professor charged with ogling women students from the bottom of the campus swimming pool: "So, just *looking* is harassment? Good grief, that's what men are supposed to do."

In Limbaugh's second book, he does an about-face, expressing outrage at ogling. His ire is raised by an Ellen Goodman column that said the ban on gays in the military should be lifted "so that straight men will learn what it's like to be sexually ogled." Limbaugh bellows, "This flippant remark shouldn't be allowed to escape scrutiny." Two pages later, he's still fuming: "We don't need to come up with ways to ridicule and irritate our servicemen, as Ms. Goodman suggests with her inane and contemptuous ogling remark."

16. Personal Attacks

Although Limbaugh is a master of personal and ad hominem attacks, he frequently denies engaging in such verbal assaults. To Limbaugh, it's just another of the false accusations leveled against him.

LIMBAUGH: Responding to a caller who criticized his personalized attacks, Limbaugh responded with a denial: "Give me a specific example: Who, what, when, where, and what exactly did I say?" (Radio, 2/18/94)

REALITY: One hour before that call, Limbaugh was telling his audience that a 5,000-year-old man found buried in ice—pictured on the cover of *Time* magazine—was really a rival talkshow host: "This is just what Sally Jessy Raphael looks like without makeup!"

LIMBAUGH: Assailing a journalist who had criticized Richard Nixon: "Michael Gartner, . . . portraying himself as a balanced, objective journalist with years and years of experience faking events, and then reporting them as news—and doing so with the express hope of destroying General Motors in one case and destroying businesses that cut down trees, the timber industry, in another." (TV, 4/27/94)

REALITY: Gartner, the NBC News president who resigned in the wake of the staged GM truck explosion on NBC's "Dateline," had no hands-on role in that incident—nor had he expressed a hope of destroying any company, including General Motors, which buys $160 million in advertising annually from the NBC network.

LIMBAUGH: "One of the hottest com-modities on the talk-show circuit in 1993 was Sherrol Miller, a 44-year-old nurse from Louisville, Kentucky. . . . Let's just say that Ms. Miller (or is it Mr.?) claims to be a transsexual lesbian." (*Told You So*, p. 212)

 REALITY: Sherrol Miller is neither a trans-sexual nor a lesbian. As explained in the *Wall Street Journal* (5/25/93), the nurse appeared frequently on TV talkshows because she had been married to a con-man bigamist who, she learned, was gay. Limbaugh mixed her up with another talkshow guest mentioned in the same *Journal* article. In the weeks after the release of Limbaugh's book, Miller said she received "about 40 telephone messages a day from all over the country—some, she said, of a threatening nature." (*Louisville Courier-Journal*, 12/2/93) Her libel suit against Limbaugh and his publisher was settled out of court. (*Gannett News Service*, 10/12/94)

"On my shows, in my newsletters and in my books, facts are not lies, and lies are not facts. . . . I am most passionate about the truth and want to ensure its dissemination to the public." (**Told You So**, *p. 292*)

 LIMBAUGH: Denouncing a fellow conserv-ative, he said of right-wing journalist Cliff Kincaid: "He's written all kinds of pieces about how I don't go make speeches for free, for the cause. . . . He's just one more of these little gnats out there trying to sink a Boeing 747 that's leaving him in a cloud of dust." (Radio, 11/19/93)

 REALITY: Kincaid's only published piece on whether Limbaugh does speeches "for the cause" was in *Human Events* (7/27/91): "He does his bit for conservatives when the move-ment calls. He waived his fees, for instance, when he emceed at roasts for Oliver North and Paul Weyrich and addressed the National Right to Life convention."

FINEST-LOOKING SPECIMEN ON THE PLANET

In response to jokes about Limbaugh's girth, a Limbaugh defender called them "tasteless and cheap." Those terms apply well to Limbaugh's frequent disparagement of peoples' appearance or physical stature—such as Secretary of Labor Robert Reich's and Attorney General Janet Reno's. Limbaugh declared that Governor Ann Richards "was born needing her face ironed." He said that Representative Henry Gonzalez (D-TX) "was playing connect the dots with the liver spots on his face." He called Secretary of State Warren Christopher "prune face."

Limbaugh was confronted on this put-down habit when he appeared as a guest on David Letterman's show in December 1993. When Limbaugh—during an anti–Hillary Clinton spiel—said that a photo of Mrs. Clinton made her look like a Pontiac hood ornament, Letterman interjected: "And you can say that because you are the finest-looking human specimen on the planet." The audience cheered wildly. It was a rare TV moment; someone had talked back to Limbaugh. "The camera zoomed in on Rush's face as he mouthed the phrase 'hoo-boy, hoo-boy.'" wrote a TV critic. (*Dallas Morning News*, 12/20/93)

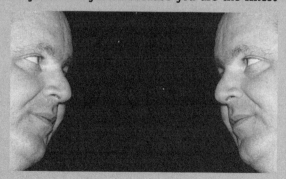

BORN-AGAIN JOE McCARTHY?

In the early 1950s, Senator Joe McCarthy used the press corps to issue a daily stream of wild, undocumented charges and Red-baiting innuendo. Today Rush Limbaugh uses his various media pulpits to broadcast charges that have more than a faint echo of the McCarthy period.

"The Peace Movement in the United States was, whether by accident or design, pro-Communist." (Limbaugh's "35 Undeniable Truths")

"I'll tell you what the environmental movement is in this country today, folks. It is the modern home of the socialist/Communist movement in America." (TV, "Earth Day Show," 4/22/93)

"Watermelons are environmentalist. They're green on the outside but red on the inside." (TV, 5/2/94)

Referring to People for the Ethical Treatment of Animals: "PETA's real mission is destroying capitalism, not saving animals." (*Ought to Be,* p. 108)

"It is neither farfetched nor unfair to draw an analogy between the civil rights leadership and the Soviet Communist leadership, insofar as exploitation of their people is concerned." (*Ought to Be,* p. 118)

On movie director Oliver Stone: "His films, whether it's *Salvador* or *Wall Street*, *Platoon*, or *JFK*, are all anti-American creeds." (*Ought to Be,* p. 260)

"Isn't it ironic that as America is celebrating its victory in the Cold War over communism, those same, tired, oppressive ideas are still winning the hearts and minds of millions of Americans?" (*Told You So,* p. 87)

Defining the issue in campaign '92: "Socialism versus America, the Democrats versus the Republicans." (Radio, 7/16/92; *The Rush Limbaugh Story,* p. 208)

Still stoking innuendo of sedition about Clinton months after he took office: "And how about that mysterious vacation to Moscow and Prague in the dead of winter?" (*Told You So,* p. 41)

"Bill Clinton may be the most effective practitioner of class warfare since Lenin. Today it's the pharmaceutical manufacturers, the cable-TV industry, insurance companies, physicians, and chief executive officers of major corporations he's targeting. Tomorrow it could be you." (*Told You So,* p. 54)

"There are many left-wing extremists now running the executive branch of the federal government. There's . . . Chairwoman of the Council of Economic Advisers Laura D'Andrea Tyson, who marvels at the wonders of Eastern European–style central planning and collectivism." (*Told You So,* p. 40)

On the authors of this book: FAIR is a "far-left media attack-dog group" (*USA Today,* 7/6/94) that attacked a TV movie because it was "too tough on Communists." (Radio, 7/5/94)

Conclusion:
Limbaugh's "Liberal Media"

Although our litany of Limbaugh falsities and fallacies could have gone on and on, we felt that roughly 100 examples would make our point. We do not mean to imply either that Limbaugh's errors are limited to these examples or that the Limbaugh story is in any way small or trivial.

A couple of years ago, the meteoric rise of a blustery charlatan from local radio host to national political power might have sounded like the stuff of Hollywood fiction: a self-styled know-it-all who displays his ignorance on a daily basis—and still amasses a following of millions. But, unlike the right-wing folksinger who strums his way into the U.S. Senate in the movie *Bob Roberts,* Limbaugh is no fictional character. Only his facts are fiction.

That a character like Limbaugh could ascend to the apex of media influence tells us much about the structure and biases of the American media. The fact that no commentator today has more broadcasting power than Limbaugh reveals the absurdity of his daily attacks on the so-called liberal media. Especially since right-wingers have long dominated opinion-shaping forums in the U.S. media: George Will, James Kilpatrick, William Safire, and William Buckley are dominant on op-ed pages; John McLaughlin, Patrick Buchanan, and Robert Novak were the first political pundits to appear daily on national TV.

RIGHT TALK RADIO

The roots of the Limbaugh story go back to the beginnings of talk radio. In the last three decades—even in liberal cities—station managers repeatedly turned over the microphone to conservative talkshow hosts hawking backlash . . . against civil rights, feminism, the peace movement. In Los Angeles, listeners have been deluged since the 1960s by a steady flood of right-wing voices: Joe Pyne, Ray Briem, Bruce Herschensohn, etc. In New York, talk radio's tone has long been set by the raging bigotry of Bob Grant, host of the biggest show on the country's biggest talk station, WABC. Limbaugh's recent rants against "long-haired, maggot-infested, dope-smoking peace pansies" may have been partly in jest—but they echoed the discourse that permeated talkshows in the previous decades. So busy attacking every type of progressive grass-roots activist, there's one group conservative hosts could be counted on *not* to criticize: big business.

Talk radio executives have always claimed that they are ready to hire any and all provocative talk hosts who could attract and hold listeners. Nice rhetoric—unfortunately, it's rarely been true. During the upsurge of massive movements for social change, radio executives didn't rush to hire the Ralph Naders, Gloria Steinems, Julian Bonds, or Abbie Hoffmans. While there was always a mike for the backlashers to those movements, frontlashers need not apply. While conservatives were allowed to use the airwaves day after day to "name the names" of activists alleged to be subversives or "commies," a progressive host might name the names of corporations ripping off the public—and that's forbidden, especially if the companies might be advertisers or station owners.

In the 1980s, talk radio boomed as a *national* format, aided by satellite technology and toll-free 800 numbers. Many conserva-

tives—some having been tried and tested in local venues—were given shots at a nationwide audience. Mort Downey Jr. jumped from local talk radio to TV stardom and, after a fall, returned to national talk radio. Those with nationally syndicated shows include convicted Watergate conspirator G. Gordon Liddy, commentator Patrick Buchanan, and Michael Reagan, conservative son of the former president. Limbaugh was just one of many rightists given a shot at a national audience, and he succeeded far beyond the others.

For all his appeal to listeners, the Limbaugh success story would have been unthinkable if he had had different enemies. Imagine that instead of targeting environmentalists, vegetarians, gays, feminists, and the homeless, Limbaugh beat up every day on major corporations and other monied interests—getting his facts wrong time and again. It's clear he wouldn't have survived in a small market like Sacramento, let alone nationally.

Today, polling data shows that talkshow listeners are mostly conservative. That's no surprise, given the limited menu that's been offered through the years—with the overwhelming majority of politically-oriented hosts clearly right-tilting, according to the National Association of Radio Talk Show Hosts. Nor is it a surprise that most listeners are males; how many self-respecting females who believe in gender equality could stomach the offerings on many of these stations? It's obvious that if a more diverse menu of program hosts were offered, a more diverse audience would listen.

Of course, not all radio talkshow hosts are right-wing. But only a few are unabashedly left-of-center. (Texas populist Jim

Hightower and former California Governor Jerry Brown are nationally syndicated—though denied access to many of the biggest markets.) On the other hand, there are a number of centrists—usually restrained in manner of delivery, often less opinionated—who allow guests and callers from various perspectives to speak. What results is a political spectrum on most talk radio stations extending from tepid centrists to rabid rightists. Ironically, Limbaugh pretty much acknowledged this reality when he lampooned the alternative to him and fellow conservatives as "Larry Lightweight, who sits there with guests on 'both sides' of the issue and asks them questions. You never hear what Larry Lightweight thinks about anything." (*Limbaugh Letter*, 10/93)

THE SPECTRUM FROM GE TO GM

This imbalanced center-right spectrum is not found *only* in talk radio; it's prevalent throughout mainstream news media. Political pundit debates on CNN are a prime example: Red-hot rightists like Pat Buchanan, Mona Charen, and Robert Novak regularly debate Mark Shields, Al Hunt of the *Wall Street Journal,* and other lukewarm centrists whose motto could be "I'm not a leftist, but I play one on TV."

Corporate ownership and sponsorship of American broadcasting is a major factor behind the limited political spectrum among talkshow hosts and pundits—a spectrum that seems to extend from GE to GM. Typically missing are advocates for consumers, the environment, workers—those who might criticize big business. Look behind the weekend TV pundit programs, CNN debate shows, even PBS's "MacNeil/Lehrer NewsHour," and you'll

"Do you ever wake up in the middle of the night and think: 'I'm full of hot gas?'"
—David Letterman to Limbaugh ("Late Show," 12/17/93)

find two politically active corporations—General Electric and Archer Daniels Midland—sponsoring most of them.

The board of GE (which also owns TV talk channels CNBC and America's Talking) can enjoy "debates" on TV and radio with little worry that GE's practices—whether in lobbying or polluting or procuring government contracts—will be top targets for criticism. Yet day after day, "feminazis" will be pilloried, along with environmental "wackos" and assorted scapegoats.

That today's broadcasting spectrum veers right is evidenced by the about-face performed recently by far-right groups like Accuracy In Media and the Eagle Forum who had spent decades crusading for the Fairness Doctrine as a tool citizens needed to challenge bias. Now, however, with the dominance of the Limbaughs and Buchanans, these groups oppose the Fairness Doctrine. They still complain about broadcasting's "liberal bias"—but even they don't seem to believe it anymore.

No event has demonstrated the power of partisan right-wing broadcasting more than the November 1994 election. It was a triumph not just for congressional Republicans, but for Rush Limbaugh and the right-wing talk hosts and commentators who have come to dominate the national "debate." And it was a victory for Pat Robertson and the broadcast networks of the Religious Right.

Republicans won their supposed landslide with only 20 percent of the country's eligible voters, about 38 million people—Limbaugh reaches more than half that number every week. It was a campaign in which mainstream TV news focused largely on who's up and who's down in the polls. For millions of Americans, what passed for "serious discussion" of the issues is what they heard from Rush Limbaugh and Limbaugh clones on talk radio.

That's a frightening thought for anyone who believes that democracy stems from real debate—not misinformed monologues. As Thomas Jefferson wrote 200 years ago, society cannot be both "ignorant and free."

WHAT CAN BE DONE ABOUT LIMBAUGH?

What can be done about Rush Limbaugh? Here's a seven-step program:

1) *Share this book*. Limbaugh despises the word "share," which he views as liberal-speak. Place this book in the hands of Limbaugh listeners. Send it to the managers of your local Limbaugh TV or radio affiliate—putting them on notice of the kind of disinformation they, through Limbaugh, disseminate. Go to bookstores or libraries that have stocked Limbaugh's books, and ask that—in the interest of balance—they carry this one as well.

2) *Demand balance*. If your local Limbaugh TV and radio stations are among those that air right-wing partisans virtually unopposed, demand balance. If the only balance offered is the kind of waffling centrist Limbaugh lampoons as "Larry Lightweight," demand that bona fide progressive hosts be added to the lineup. Jim Hightower and Jerry Brown, for example, are available to virtually every radio station in the country.

3) *Demand redress*. Station managers are responsible for the falsehoods that they broadcast. When you hear Limbaugh distort facts, ask the station to correct the record. Many publications do it; why shouldn't broadcasters who insist on airing a talk host with a proven propensity to prevaricate? When Limbaugh attacks an individual or group, ask that response time be provided for the other side to be heard.

4) *Encourage scrutiny and debate*. The anticensorship approach to someone like Limbaugh is not to pull the plug on him, but to turn the spotlight on him and his

quackery. Write letters to the editor exposing him. Contact journalists who cover TV and radio and encourage them to scrutinize Limbaugh, his clones, and a broadcasting structure that favors right-wing voices. Encourage national TV and radio programs to examine Limbaugh's reign of error, and to challenge Limbaugh to meet his critics in public debate. Try to call Limbaugh (1-800-282-2882 during airtime) and his imitators to challenge their veracity and talk radio bias in general; if you're repeatedly blocked in getting on the air, publicize the censorship.

5) *Work for media reform.* Most of the U.S. media is today concentrated in the hands of 20 giant corporations, a structure that breeds corporate-friendly demagogues like Limbaugh. Organize politically so that antitrust principles are applied to the media, and the monopolization process is stopped; return the broadcast airwaves from a handful of companies to their legal owners, the public; resurrect truly public, truly noncommercial broadcasting; ensure public access to and democratic control over communication channels in the "information superhighway" now under construction.

6) *Support positive alternatives.* In this era of corporate-dominated media, informed citizens must seek out diverse sources of information. Subscribe to independent publications that are neither owned by giant firms nor fed by big advertisers—magazines like *The Nation*, *The Progressive*, *In These Times*, *Ms.*, *Mother Jones*, to name just a few. Support noncommercial radio, such as the Pacifica stations. Patronize bookstores and newsstands that offer diverse viewpoints.

7) *Join FAIR and subscribe to its magazine, EXTRA!* (See "About FAIR," inside cover)

Whether you use these approaches or develop your own, the key point is to stand up and be counted against ignorance and bigotry. Since mid-1994, when FAIR first challenged Limbaugh's reign of error, he's been flailing away at critics. It's a good time to keep the heat on. In the final words of his lengthy interview in *Penthouse* magazine, Limbaugh is quoted as saying: "People always panic when the jig is up." On that point, Limbaugh knows of what he speaks.

Afterword:
Limbaugh's Response to FAIR

For three and a half months, the world—and millions of ditto-heads—waited for Rush Limbaugh's promised "point-by-point rebuttal" to FAIR's original (June 1994) report exposing his "Reign of Error." On October 11, 1994, Limbaugh's response finally arrived—a 37-page manuscript so lacking in documentation that it prompted a skeptical news article in the *Washington Times* (10/11/94), one of the country's most right-wing dailies. A livid Limbaugh assailed the *Washington Times* reporter on his radio show as a "bleephead," and called his reporting "laughable."

But it was Limbaugh's response that was laughable. Neither a "rebuttal" nor "point-by-point," it dealt with only about half of the 43 claims shown to be inaccurate by FAIR. On those claims that Limbaugh did address, he offered evasions, irrelevant quotes, off-point texts, passages from opinion columnists and, in many instances, fresh distortions. He admitted only a few of his scores of errors, yet documented not one of his claims.

Forest Acreage (p. 18 of book): To defend his erroneous statement that "we have more acreage of forest land in the United States today than we did at the time the Constitution was written," the best Limbaugh could do was to cite a statistic that favorably compared forest acreage today to that in 1920—133 years too late.

Student Loans (p. 23): Limbaugh managed only a half-hearted defense of his silly comment that "banks take risks in issuing student loans" (in fact, they're federally guaranteed). He quoted a bankers' association official saying the "risk" is that the government won't reimburse unpaid loans if the banks don't follow proper procedures—a novel use of the concept of "risk" in lending.

American Indian Population (p. 48): Unable to find a source to support his assertion that "there are more American Indians alive today than there were when Columbus arrived," he served up a quote from the Heritage Foundation's magazine that "some Indian groups are more populous today than in 1492."

Anita Hill's "Dating" (p. 53) Lacking evidence for his absurd claim that Anita Hill "wanted to continue to date" Clarence Thomas, Limbaugh substituted bravado, instead. "My comment about Hill dating Thomas," wrote Limbaugh, "actually demonstrates my recall of the Thomas-Hill episode." And then he offered a long excerpt from David Brock's Hill-bashing book that doesn't mention dating at all; it only cites Thomas—who has never claimed they dated—saying that Hill had invited him into her home after Thomas had driven her home from work.

U.S. Health Care Superiority (p. 65): In the face of statistics showing the United States ranking below almost all industrialized nations in life expectancy and infant mortality, Limbaugh continued to insist that our health care system was superior, because those two measures "have almost nothing to do with the quality of American medical care." Yet those are the very two measures he uses in *See, I Told You So* (p. 153) to prove that U.S. health is constantly improving.

In his "rebuttal," Limbaugh argued (quoting Elizabeth McCaughey) that these two statistics merely "reflect the epidemic

LIMBAUGH: On the *Washington Post* article about FAIR's report on "Limbaugh's Reign of Error": "Howard Kurtz of the *Washington Post* called us for reaction. And we gave them a full-page, substantive response. They ran one sentence." (*Limbaugh Letter,* 9/94)

of low-birth-weight babies born to teenage and drug-addicted mothers, as well as the large numbers of homicides in American cities and drug-related deaths." In fact, infant mortality is closely linked to the amount of prenatal care given to expectant mothers. And homicides, according to the Centers for Disease Control, lower U.S. life expectancy only by about three months—which would hardly improve the U.S. ranking.

Canadian Doctors (p. 66): To show a basis for his claim that "most Canadian physicians who are themselves in need of surgery . . . scurry across the border to get it done right," Limbaugh provided three off-point pages of rebuttal text. The pages contain no evidence of a single Canadian doctor seeking surgery in the U.S.—let alone "most"—though there's evidence of Canadian doctors seeking *work* in the United States. Limbaugh solves the problem by passing off his book passage as "an obvious humorous exaggeration." You can look up the perfectly straightforward assertion on page 153 of *See, I Told You So*.

Chelsea's School (p. 71): It's clear that even Limbaugh knows that CBS News never reported the story that Sidwell Friends, Chelsea Clinton's school, had required students to write an essay on "Why I Feel Guilty Being White," and that a CBS infotainment sheet had clearly lifted the (third-hand) story from *Playboy*. Limbaugh's response to FAIR trumpeted the fact that he had finally found a more original source for the story: The "Why I Feel Guilty Being White" essay title originally appeared in an article in D.C.'s *City Paper* (7/16/93). "My office did what no journalist did," Limbaugh boasted. "We tracked the story to its root, and talked to the original reporter. He confirmed the story."

But as Limbaugh knows full well, his office was not the first to call the *City Paper* reporter, Bill Gifford. The September/October issue of FAIR's magazine *EXTRA!* had mentioned Gifford's article—

 REALITY: The *Post* article (7/1/94) included not one but five sentences from the Limbaugh response; the one-page response offered not a single substantive word defending the truth of any of Limbaugh's claims.

and noted that his anonymous source, a disgruntled parent, was now waffling, saying the essay assignment was something like "Should White People Feel Guilty?" Unlike Limbaugh, FAIR tracked the story to its real root—the Sidwell Friends school—and discovered that there was no evidence that any such essay had been assigned.

Limbaugh's lie that the *City Paper* reporter stood by the original story about the essay was exposed by the *Washington Post* (10/18/94) and even by the *Washington Times* (10/11/94)—leading to a memorable rant by Limbaugh against reporters who check information before publishing it. (Radio, 10/11/94)

James Madison Quote (p. 80): Limbaugh admitted that he was mistaken in attributing a quote to James Madison that Americans should "sustain ourselves according to the Ten Commandments of God." But he went on to argue that "fully documented quotes by Madison" said pretty much the same thing. In fact, the quotes of Madison provided by Limbaugh largely argue for the separation of church and state—which is the exact opposite of the point Limbaugh had been making with the bogus quote.

Iran-Contra (p. 81): On his false claim that no one had been indicted in the Iran-Contra scandal, Limbaugh declared: "I obviously misspoke when I said there were no indictments—I clearly meant to say there were no *convictions*, a point I have made on many occasions."

But Limbaugh did not "misspeak": He had argued at length (TV, 1/19/94) that no Iran-Contra indictment had occurred. And his fallback position of "no convictions" was also false: Of the 14 indictments, most resulted in convictions or guilty pleas, including many felonies. That's why Limbaugh was already backpedaling in his rebuttal document, going on to claim there were "no convictions on the substantive points."

PRINTING BOTH SIDES IS UNFAIR REPORTING

Denouncing biased practices at one of America's most right-wing dailies: "We sent out over 150, maybe 200, copies of this [37-page response to FAIR's report] to various columnists, newspapers which had printed the FAIR report originally and so forth. To this date, only one newspaper, the **Washington Times,** *has sought to do a story on my response. And the way that it happened was laughable. We sent our response out, a reporter from the* **Washington Times** *gets it, and immediately calls FAIR and says: 'What do you think of this?' They then call us*

Gulf War (p. 84): On his claim that the U.S. Congress opposed the Gulf War, Limbaugh admitted that "Congress eventually went along with President Bush's policy—but they had to be dragged along, kicking and screaming." This was different from his original response to FAIR, given on his radio show (7/5/94): "They claim that I said the only institutions who did not support George Bush in the Gulf War were the United States Congress, the United States House, and Senate. . . . I did say that, and when I said it, it was true." Sheer deception. Limbaugh's original claim had been made on April 18, 1994—more than three years after Congress authorized the use of force in the Gulf.

Whitewater Coverage (p. 91): Implying a media cover-up, the self-styled Whitewater expert had said in February 1994 that he couldn't recall a single front-page story on Whitewater in the *New York Times*—the paper that had broken the story on its front page in March 1992. His rebuttal complained: "The fact that I overlooked one *Times* article that ran 11 months earlier is hardly indicative of a 'reign of error.'" Still more errors reigned. He'd overlooked not one but more than a half-dozen front-page *Times* stories on Whitewater; the first had run 23 months earlier, not eleven.

Limbaugh's evasions would be comical if it were not for his dead-serious devotees, many of whom are eager to accept his absurd claims—even when they are self-contradictory.

As Limbaugh likes to say, usually when he's dissecting Bill Clinton's doubletalk: "Words mean things!"

and say: 'All right, here's what FAIR thinks of your response. What do you think of what they said?' And we got on the phone and we said, 'Listen bleep-head, you have our response in your hands, that's all you're going to get. Run our response!' That's what I think is called for here. We're not going to get into a tit-for-tat, blow-by-blow. It's not the point. The point is we've responded to these charges, you have them in their hands and there they are." (Radio, 10/11/94. **The Washington Times did not print a news story on FAIR's original report.**)

CONTRIBUTORS/ ACKNOWLEDGMENTS/ CREDITS

Contributors: John Canham-Clyne, Neil DeMause, Jonathan Eagleman, Carolyn Francis, Doug Henwood, and Miranda Spencer.

We offer special thanks to our fellow staffers at FAIR for their contributions to this book: Janine Jackson, Sam Husseini, Hollie Ainbinder, Geralyn Byers, Tiffany Devitt, Laura Flanders, and Dan Shadoan. We also thank FAIR researchers and associates for their help, especially Matthew Amster, Kristen Fayne-Mulroy, Angus Grieve-Smith, Anna Gullberg-Lundkvist, Helen Hamblin, Martin Lee, Scott Marcus, and Norman Solomon.

This book benefitted from the work of independent investigators and writers: Brian Keliher, editor of the *Flush Rush Quarterly (FRQ)* and author of *Flush Rush;* David Barsamian of "Alternative Radio"; Michael Corman; Professor Don Lazere and his students at Cal Poly San Luis Obispo; Joshua Shenk of *The New Republic;* and Don Trent Jacobs, author of *The Bum's Rush*.

INDEX